LIVING ON TICK

103

*Tales from a Huddersfield
Corner Shop between
the Wars*

LIVING ON TICK

*Tales from a Huddersfield
Corner Shop between
the Wars*

Hazel Wheeler

TEMPUS

First published 2002
Copyright © Hazel Wheeler, 2002

Tempus Publishing Limited
The Mill, Brimscombe Port,
Stroud, Gloucestershire, GL5 2QG

ISBN 0 7524 2616 8

Typesetting and origination by
Tempus Publishing Limited
Printed in Great Britain by
Midway Colour Print, Wiltshire

Frontispiece: *Joe Taylor at the door of his shop in the 1930s*

Contents

For Audrey, Philip, Granville and all those who enriched my life with so much laughter and love.

Until the dawn breaks and the shadows flee…

ONE

Living On Tick

⚜

Living 'on tick' was a way of life for some of our customers at Central Stores. Bad debts accumulated from year to year until death wafted the consumer to a mode of existence that didn't depend on how many goods her local grocer would allow her to have and 'pay next week' – if he was lucky.

On the 'never-never' was an apt description. An old order book from March 1922, black with dust and age, was found in the attic of Central Stores when it was converted to a private house in the 1970s by new owners. In Joe's handwriting (my dad) it proves his 'logic' that if he refused to allow a certain amount 'on tick' he would lose a customer. They would go elsewhere, leaving him with outstanding bills. Whereas if they kept patronising his shop he was making a profit, despite the weekly balance always left over till next week.

It must have been mildly infuriating, however, having to listen to some of the feeble reasons for withholding payment. 'Well tha sees lad, t'doctor has to be paid,' was a regular excuse. Apparently, it was quite alright to keep a tradesman waiting for his money, but a professional man had first claim on wages. They didn't realise that if the grocer refused them food, then it would not be a doctor they would be needing but an undertaker. Some even had the cheek to say they'd spent a bit at't Co-op to get some 'divvy' and they wouldn't let them have tick there. But they needed the divvy to save up for Whitsuntide new shoes or a wireless set.

The type of commodities on the weekly shopping list – and how much they cost are shown on the order book. All the customers had coal fires for heating the house with and for cooking on Yorkshire ranges as well. Walter Thomas's order reflected those needs. He bought

Hilda and Joe Taylor, before their marriage, on a visit to Annie Whitworth's at Moldgreen in 1922

3d of matches, tapers 3d. Sugar cost him 2/-, cheese 9d, rice 6d. Rice, of course, was only for rice puddings in those days. The era of long grain rice for first course meals had yet to reach our Deighton village.

Walter ordered corned beef (a good old standby) 7d, biscuits 11½ d, flour 2/11d. Lots of people made their own bread, so yeast was a regular item on grocery orders. Walter had five pennyworth. Then a bottle of sauce for 10 ½ d and salt 2d. Besides having chips with everything, if they fancied them, people had salt with everything as well, and never thought a thing about it. Indeed, diets never entered anyone's head, they took everything with a pinch of salt so to speak. Whatever they may have worried about, their figures certainly didn't seem to be one of them.

Central Stores stocked just about every necessity of life, from food to cleaning materials. Walter also had a donkey stone on that week's order, 1½ d, a packet of Rinso washing powder 3½ d, starch 3d, soap ½ d. Stockings for Mrs Thomas, 3/-, a pudding basin 5 ½ d. It would be white or brown ware, Pyrex wasn't known then at our shop. Walter also wanted a reel of cotton 5d – they were good customers and paid on the dot. On 3 March 1922 their bill totalled £1 11s 6d.

Mrs Corbett, on the other hand, believed in 'leaving a few bob over' each week, making her own decision how much she would pay. How galling it must have been, handing goods over the counter and never knowing when they would be paid for! It wasn't the poorest who were the worst payers either. That week she already had a balance from the previous one of 3/8 ½. So it headed the list before the new items were entered of tea 10d, sugar 1/6d, sausage 7½ d, ham shank (a great standby with mushy peas to fill hungry Yorkshire bellies), a good buy at 1/4d. It was turned over in a customer's hands a few times, to ascertain how much meat there still was left on. Mrs Corbett's bacon for the week cost 1/1d.

In 1923 mother arrived on the scene and she would occasionally throw out a sarcastic remark about a customer still being able to afford to smoke. To which the usual retort would be 'nay, we've got to 'ave us fags lass.' Though family businesses then ran on the lines that 'the customer is always deemed to be right', one had to be something of a diplomat and master of tact, besides acting as a marriage guidance counsellor when rifts occurred in the marital state of customers. The village grocer ministered to most of their wants, temporal and spiritual until Sunday came round once more. The popular village grocer must be all things to all his customers, even acting as a stand-up comic if they were feeling 'a bit down'.

Joe may have passed his Cambridge Junior, and yearned to be something more than a village grocer, but the customers certainly benefited from his quick wit and outgoing personality. What a mental arithmetic marvel he was too! He could 'tot up' prices of whole rows of goods in his head, quick as lightening. A late Huddersfield mathematical genius, Ruth Lawrence, would have had a job to match his arithmetical ability. No such things as computers and ready reckoners then, shop assistants either added it up in their heads or jotted the pounds, shillings and pence on a scrap of paper behind the counter.

Mrs Parkin was another customer in that week of March 1922. She needed a new frying pan, so bought one from 'Joe's' for 2/3d.

A page from Dad's customers' order book for 1922.

9

Also on her order was the ever popular HP Sauce at $10\frac{1}{2}$ d and a Bermaline loaf, 6d, the malty-coloured, soft loaf with a wrapper round the middle which was a teatime favourite in the twenties and thirties. With a bit of cheese it made a perfectly adequate and tasty tea. Her ordinary loaf cost four pence. Our grocery shop also sold fruit and vegetables – Mrs Parkin bought bananas for 8d and 'Cigs' at 6d. Sometimes items were lumped together under the words 'Goods' but that could be a bit tricky with some, who might dispute they had ever had any 'goods'. Mrs Parkin also bought a tin of salmon, 1/5d. Altogether the shopping amounted to £1 14s 2d and she paid one pound, leaving quite a hefty balance of 14/2d.

Mrs Saunders was another customer who lived on tick. Before she even began leaning her elbows on the counter top and deciding what she required that week, there was £1 13s 0d left over from the week before. Undeterred she piled on more: Cocoa $8\frac{1}{2}$d; six eggs, 2/-; candles 2d; pork $3/4\frac{1}{2}$d. There were no refrigerators, but we did have long, dangling fly catching papers swinging from the ceiling which were sometimes covered with flies in hot weather.

Food was only eaten in season then, and so pork would be alright because, according to superstition, there was an 'R' in the month. Mrs Saunders also needed new stockings, 2/2d, a handkerchief 6d (paper tissues also a thing of the future), so having a bad cold meant a lot of extra washing. It must have been a nuisance in wintry weather to have lots of wet steaming handkerchiefs drying over the creel.

Then Mrs Saunders ordered Sloane's liniment at 2/-, hair-

A penny greetings card of the sort sold at Central Stores.

grips, 10d, matches 4d, Beechams powders 2d, and fancied a Sally Lunn, another 6d. These were huge iced buns. She didn't forget twist for her husband to smoke, $\frac{1}{4}$d and firewood. Had Mrs Saunders been concerned about not paying her bill in full, she could have done without that last item for a start, and gone into the nearby woods to gather sticks to light her fire. To her generation buying bundles of firewood meant 'instant' fires.

Joe, and anyone else who may be about when Mrs Heaton entered the shop, quailed and hung about in the back kitchen hoping someone else would go in and serve. Always in sensible wrapover pinafore and greying hair in steel curlers, she cut a formidable figure. She addressed mother as 'Bones' and she pronounced it 'Booans'. 'Na Booans' was her greeting should mother go to serve her, taking her remark more as a compliment than anything, as flattened chests were all the rage among 'Flappers' in the twenties.

That week in March, Mrs Heaton bought eight pennyworth of stamps (yes, the shop acted as post office too – we also sold birthday cards). Customers used to pore over the verses for ages wondering which verse would be most appropriate. Ponderously mouthing the words out loud, weighing up the appropriate sentiments for father, sister or cousin. They were single, shiny cards with embossed borders. They were kept in a long box and cost, maybe a penny each.

Mrs Heaton's teatime favourite was potted meat, she bought four pennyworth; six oranges at 1d each and a hairnet, 6d – like the late Ena Sharples, she was never without one, even after her curlers had been taken out. Cold cream on her order was 2d, corned beef, a 'regular' on most customer's weekly orders – Mrs Heaton had three pennyworth. When the goods amounted to £1 6s 3d, she remembered she wanted some bacon and that was another 11d. She regally handed over £1 2s 6d, leaving an even larger balance that week than before.

In a way, I suppose, the knowledge that Joe was 'nobbut down t' street' (or up) it was a kind of social security for those people of the 1920s. They knew full well that whatever happened, he would never allow any one of them to go short of food. Even if his own creditors occasionally had to remind him that a bill was still outstanding.

As some try and fiddle the DHSS today, some of those customers tried fiddles with the village shopkeeper. Swearing blind it was a pound note they had handed over, not a ten shilling one, or a half crown instead of a florin or two shillings. So the shopkeeper had to remember to put the money on top of the till to prove beyond doubt what amount had been paid over the counter. Some customers had the cheek to demand the coins returned for handing back pop and soda water bottles, yet still left a balance on their bill. 'Pop' bottles at least saved the litter of tin cans and the incentive was there to return them to the shop.

Apart from that, life changes little really – but the prices do.

TWO

The Lamplighter Man

In these days of technology, few will remember gas lamps or seeing the lamplighter man with his long pole of office approaching down the road on long winter evenings. Lamplighters are probably already as forgotten as the muffin man, the yeast man and the chimney sweep with his sooty face.

The late Norman Keely, who came to Huddersfield in 1913, first worked for George Hall, wholesale grocer, as a barrow boy. When the First World War was over, jobs were scarce. But in 1923 Norman heard that a lamplighter was required by Huddersfield Corporation. 'Do you pay your rates?' asked the chap who interviewed him. 'Yes' replied Norman, wondering why such a question was asked. 'Well then, you're entitled to a job' replied Mr Riley.

So Norman acquired the regulation heavy blue overcoat of Melton cloth, with the proud words 'Huddersfield Corporation Lamp Department' inscribed on the collar. He also had a pair of waders, and the outfit was supposed to last five years. The pole was 7 ft long, a steel tube with brass fittings at the top. There was a hole one inch wide where the calder oil and petrol was put in. Gas lamps were not as high as the present electric ones. Besides the vessel containing petrol, Norman carried a drop of petrol on his rounds as well.

Every Tuesday the town's lamplighters were given two dozen new gas mantles and allowed four boxes of matches weekly – windy nights were worse than snow for a lamplighter, when he could use four boxes a night! In summertime boxes were 'put by' to keep in a good stock for winter.

Does ayone remember the old music hall ditty, 'Oh, it's a windy night tonight, tonight, oh, it's a windy night tonight, tonight. The wind keeps

Norman Keely, ex-lamplighter outside his home in Sheepridge, 1973.

blowing round the houses, I can feel it blowing up me trousers…' – bet Norman had that sensation many a time, but he kept a cheery grin on his face.

Wash leathers were supplied for cleaning the lamps and expected to last for a couple of months. Besides lighting up in an evening, then extinguishing the lamps in the morning, Norman used to spend four hours cleaning the lamps – Monday to Friday, beginning at nine o'clock and finishing at one. Afternoons were his own until lighting up time and it was a seven days a week job. On Tuesdays and Fridays lamplighters had to report any damages.

During the twenties, Huddersfield Corporation employed fifty or sixty lamplighters. Lamps were situated at corners, over dark passages and outside shops. We had one on the cobbled square outside Central Stores. It was marvellous for playing out with the illumination on autumn and winter evenings and for playing 'Relievo' – touch the lamp post and you were safe. Some lads enjoyed scrimming up the post and hanging from the rail.

A lamplighter's wages were about 25/- a week. Perks were 'thank you' gifts from appreciative citizens at Christmas time. Outside Newhouse Hall was a 'paid lamp' for which the owner, Mr T.P. Crossland, paid the Corporation a shilling a year. The housemaid at the Hall always gave Norman half a crown at Christmas.

He never had time to stop for refreshment, having to keep to a rigid time-table. Many will have heard the story about the spirit of a dog, said to occasionally appear in Newhouse Wood, by the Hall. More than once, when Norman was lighting that paid lamp, he heard a sudden 'swoosh' and the shape of a big white dog flashed by, usually on or around

Christmas Eve. Norman also claimed to have seen the white clad figure of a young woman, gazing idly out of an upstairs window in Newhouse Hall. One murky morning in mid-winter he was homeward bound after putting the gas lamps out. Suddenly a voice boomed, 'You've got a good coat on lad, tha'd better give it to me'. Being only a small chap Norman deemed discretion the better part of valour, as the figure confronting him was large and muscular. He completed the walk home shivering and coatless. A few days later he found it, wet through, in a field.

There were vandals in those days too. One evening Norman was enjoying a cup of cocoa when an urgent knocking called him to the door. 'Come quickly', pleaded the woman on his doorstep, 'some lads have put a little kitten in one of your lamps'. When he reached the scene the poor little creature was pacing round and round the hot gas mantle, with frantic movements and pleading eyes. Norman scrimmed up the lamp post, opened the glass window and with a 'meow' of thanks the kitten leapt gracefully to the ground.

While on his rounds Norman whiled away the hours singing snatches of popular songs. Rather nonsensical but many with a haunting Al Jolsen melody. One of his favourites was 'Wheezy Anna, where the bugs wear clogs, Oo my, can't you hear the crickets calling? Calling for me and you, when the moon is shining and my heart is pining. Meet me where the sugar cane grows'.

To prevent his hands cracking in frosty weather, he used to rub taller over them before going out. Frequently, the last lamp lit, he saw the village 'bobby'. The couple enjoyed a fish and a penn'orth together. Norman thought that the 'coppers' of the 1920's had the right answer to delinquents. 'If he saw 'em doing

Annie Whitworth with her box Brownie camera in the garden of Central Stores in 1921.

15

owt wrong, he'd give 'em a good clout there and then. The lads only had to see the constable's lamp hanging on his belt, which he twisted round so that the glare of the light fell full on the culprit's face, and that was enough.'

To mark his years as a lamplighter, Norman had a framed testimonial in pride of place in his bungalow at Wiggan Lane, Sheepridge. A bungalow he bought with a thirty pounds deposit in the 1930s.

He retained happy memories of those bygone years when, with his lamplighter's pole and a cheery smile and happy song he helped shed a ray of light in a dark Huddersfield wintry world.

'Lead, Kindly Light', could well have been a hymn dedicated to such as he, 'Amid the encircling gloom. The night is dark, and I am far from home, lead thou me on.'

THREE

The Infants' School

It was during my infants' class days that it first dawned on me how being in a better off position than most of my contemporaries could be both beneficial and detrimental at one and the same time. I could use my advantages and riches, i.e. easily accessible sweets from our shop, to consolidate friendships after falling out, or the threats of victimisation by bullies. Some lads often threatened to 'knock my block off' if I failed to smuggle them a few humbugs, aniseed balls, marbles, or whatever it was they demanded.

The elementary school with its infants' section was a few yards further up the hill from our shop. On that first morning in 1931, I began school aged four years – mother dressed me warmly in fleecy-lined liberty bodice, vest, navy knickers, woollen green jersey and tartan plaid skirt, the flap held together by an enormous, shiny safety pin. The elastic in the legs of my knickers dug into my flesh and I'd keep twanging it away from my thighs for relief. De rigueur in those days was a pocket in school knickers for keeping handkerchiefs in. Though some brought pet mice instead, hidden away there until found by a horrified teacher. I preferred to put my hankie in my cardigan pocket rather than fumble up my knickers every time I needed it. Some children kept a few toffees there, for playtime.

My first impressions of the infants' classroom were of clouds of chalk dust floating about everywhere. Cardboard boxes lay around the room full of whole or broken bits of pink, blue, yellow, green and white chalk. A blackboard was fixed all the way round the room and check dusters festooned window ledges and the teacher's desk. One girl had the honour of being the ink monitor, going round with a big jar of Stephenson's ink, topping up the ink wells.

Everything was in miniature. I was especially enthusiastic about the infants' lavatories which were at the far end of the playground. Nothing

Deighton Elementary school in about 1930, from a postcard photograph taken by the author's uncle and sold at Central Stores for ½d.

so futuristic as indoor ones in the early thirties. They were almost as low as chamber pots and when we had to be 'excused' from lessons we darted across the yard to them. In the mid winter sitting on one was, what I imagined it must be like, sitting on top of an iceberg in the middle of the Atlantic Ocean. Almost as bad as the icy cold was the fear of having one's way barred by a little boy – a youthful flasher determined to see what girls had to flash too.

Perhaps fear of those lads was the reason for the number of 'accidents' that occurred on the classroom floor. A four or five year old was timorous enough already of putting up a hand to say 'Please miss, can I be excused?' When being excused might entail a tussle with a big boy trying to pull one's knickers down again while the Arctic winds howled around, doing it where one sat probably seemed the lesser of two evils for some of the infants.

Often I had to put my feet at odd angles to escape an ever-widening puddle emerging from beneath the desk next to mine. Then one of the infants would be dispatched to fetch the caretaker, who bustled in with mop, bucket and sawdust. The culprit was ordered to go and wash his or her undergarments, then bring them back and hang them over the pipes to dry. Some teachers in those days were such martinets, installing terror into their charges, so much that they themselves brought on these bladder lapses, by fear alone. The very fact that the little one knew that certain teachers refused to allow them to 'go across the yard' during lesson time was enough to trigger off the impulse. So most days there were little clouds of steam rising up from the hot water pipes against the walls, where a miniature pair of knickers or underpants had a race with the big, round-faced clock on the wall. Would they be dry by home time?

Physical Education was called drill when I was an infant. Even then I felt a deep humiliation when being ordered to leap about, touch my toes, stre-e-e-etch, then attempt feeble leap frogs over another child's bent back, with my jumper tucked into an ungainly heap down my knickers. My body felt to be entirely bereft of any kind of propeller for such antics. Those who did manage to leap over must have had no mother at home warning them, 'be careful you don't break your neck now', when they knew it was a drill morning. Or could it have been the less than aesthetic nature of the exercise – those girl infants looking to me like so many leaping pumpkins out there in the chilly school yard, that inhibited my prowess. Indeed, passing villagers frequently leaned their arms over the school wall and passed a few minutes watching our cavorting forms.

Deighton Council school, early 1930s, with Hazel Taylor in the second row, fifth from the right.

Hazel Taylor at age six years.

Miss Walker was such a martinet, in Paisley-flowered smock, brown brogues, and pepper and salt hair scraped back into a firm, uncompromising bun at the nape of her slim neck. Even today, if ever I think about her, I automatically see, in my mind's eye, rows and rows of those team bands over her arms and a cardboard box full of squashy bean bags. They were used for races, those bands. Teams were split up into dark green bands, blue red or yellow. Some of the children became really ferocious if we missed a pass, as if there was a million pounds at stake at the end of it all. Instead of a 'Well done greens', or whatever, from Miss Walker. But worst of all terrors and indignities was when Miss Walker, ruler in hand, rhythmically tapping it against her thigh, demanded we turn somersaults on the dingy grey, rectangular mat out in the yard. Mother forbade such daredevil pranks at home – not that we would ever try them – saying we'd get our necks twisted round the wrong way and never get them right again. I certainly didn't feel like throwing away my hardly-begun life for the sake of Miss Walker and her whims.

Reluctant somersaulters were woman-handled over the mat, with impatient calls from somewhere above. 'Tuck your head in, tuck your head in and don't be such a ninny!' Ooh, the hate that oozed out of one ninny as I tried to roll sideways in a pseudo somersault! It crossed my mind that maybe Miss Walker herself had never done a somersault and could have been similarly browbeaten by a teacher years ago. This was her revenge. Anyhow, I had such nightmares about drill day that eventually mother asked dad to send Miss Walker a letter, asking for me to be excused. 'I didn't go through nine months for the result to be twisted into non recognition through stupid somersaults', mother said.

Even so, that didn't absolve me from sums. They were always the first course on the infant school menu after assembly and hymn singing. I couldn't see the point in learning multiplication tables. I would live at our shop forever and would never need to go shopping myself. Food and every other necessity of life (even nit combs) would somehow just come to me through the shop door. It never dawned on me for ages that dad or grandad had to pay for the stuff first before we had anything for our customers to buy from us.

Playtimes at school were either happy, or a brief interlude to get over as quickly as possible. I didn't like the little bottles of milk with cardboard tops we had to drink first. Or the clouded empty bottles standing in their crates when we'd finished. If my particular friends were all present I felt safe. We played at skipping and 'running-in'. I wasn't particularly good at that, but when I did manage it successfully without becoming hopelessly entangled in the rope, the glow of achievement lasted throughout the day. Life then depended, or seemed to depend, on whether or not I was a good runner in. Sometimes we played exercises; various permutations against the school wall with an India rubber ball. Throwing it against the wall, clapping our hands quickly before it returned to us, bouncing, twirling round, catching the ball, throwing a leg over it – one, two three alara – four, five, six, alara... all manner of crazes were thought up. Ditties to chant while we skipped, panting and red faced:

> *I am a Girl Guide dressed in blue*
> *These are the actions I must do*
> *Salute to the King*
> *Curtsey to the Queen*
> *And turn my back to the dirty machine*

If we'd had to do all the energetic carrying on for a living we'd have gone on strike, I'm sure. I didn't really enjoy playing 'It'. Being chased all over the concrete yard by whoever was 'It'. Swerving here and there to avoid being captured, bumping heads with other children, usually ending up on my knees in a bloody mess. Rising, close to tears, with black grit sticking in open wounds and bright red blood pouring terrifyingly out of them.

A big girl from one of the older classes would be on first aid duty in the cloakroom. Injured knees and grazed hands were first washed then iodine was applied. That was when I learned to keep a stiff upper lip. In a way it was a relief to be among the stiff jointed, bandaged brigade, it was my absolution from further violent games or gymnastics for a while.

There were other trials. Betty, the farmer's daughter, stood next to me for singing lessons. Her fingers were never happy unless they were plucking all the lovely, pale blue fluff from my angora cardigan or nipping my flesh wherever she could find an exposed bit. It hurt but no matter how often she was caned, she never overcame her addiction. One could always tell exactly where I'd been standing in the singing lesson, by the pile of blue fluff on the wooden floorboards.

Mother was in the happy position of being able to pop into town to the wholesale drapers and order whatever she wanted. Including lots of pretty clothes for me. You see she didn't have to hand over ready cash, so in a way it felt as though she wasn't having to pay. Indirectly I suppose, such as Betty the farmer's daughter were jealous of my clothes, so took it out on me by trying to pull them to pieces.

When any of the children were sent to the headmaster to be caned the teacher went also. The rest of us went deathly quiet, listening intently with a kind of vicarious thrill as we heard the swish of the punishment ruler come down.

One male teacher used to fondle my bare legs as I stood by his desk waiting for him to mark my exercise book. I thought that made me teachers pet and though I wished he wouldn't, I looked upon it as a

Deighton Council school, 1920s.

mark of affection. At least he wasn't shouting at me, like he did with the boys.

What a relief when home time arrived. If we dashed noisily to the door where freedom beckoned when the bell clanged we were immediately sent back to our desks. Then made to wait, hands on heads, for a whole minute in complete silence.

Oh, how I envied Grandad's hens, when I burst in through the shop door after school and out of the back kitchen to see them. There they were in the henyard, scratching about contentedly, clucking and crowing, not a care in the world. No multiplication tables to furrow their brows, or horrible somersaults to distort their natural contours. I wished with all my heart after a particularly upsetting day at school – cardigan being picked to pieces, nine times table, big boys chasing me, that God would turn me into one of our hens and let me stay at home forever – providing that I'd be allowed to come inside when it was dark at bedtime.

The cock's authoritarian crowing, which I sometimes heard as we played in the school yard, was most reassuring to me. 'Don't worry Hazel' it seemed to crow confidently, 'you're near enough to make a dash for home if events prove too much for you'. If I looked over the school wall sometimes I saw mother in the back garden of the shop, hanging out lines full of her artificial silk stockings. If it was arithmetic lesson next I envied those, blowing so freely in the wind.

Every afternoon infants had to endure an enforced rest period. We'd hoist ourselves up onto small wooden tables, put a small hassock beneath our heads, and 'keep them down'. I worried in case the hassock had previously been used by one of the children who had nits in her hair and found it impossible to rest. I never have been able to relax among a lot of people, let alone sleep in broad daylight and in public. Especially with a teacher tip-toeing between the tables to make sure we had our eyes shut. Mine flickered constantly. I felt that someone had to keep a weather eye open lest any of the recumbent forms rolled over onto the floor, it would be a long way down.

There were some aspects of infant school that I adored, however. Not the exhibitionists who, come the first shaft of spring sunshine, spent long hours practising hand stands against the school walls, and cartwheels, but the last half hour of Friday afternoons. It was then we had private reading. In the corner of the classroom, covered with a pull on, chintzy curtain, were a couple of shelves of books. We could choose one and read it

Empire Day pageant at Deighton Council school, c. 1930.

for that precious half hour before the home time bell went. That was one of the times when I would more than willingly have stayed after hours to see what happened next in my fairy story. Yet even that happy half hour could occasionally be disconcerting if ginger-haired Dorothy, who sat at the desk in front of me, had had another invasion of lice. Her hand kept flashing through the thick, straight hair, which was cut short, pudding bowl style and I hoped her nits weren't good jumpers.

Every evening, after tea, mother went through the tense ritual of combing my hair with a specially made black comb. Black so the fawn coloured nits would show up better. We sold these combs in the shop, and there was quite a roaring undercover trade for them during the early thirties. It was always a hush-hush transaction. No customer ever asked for one if another person was waiting to be served. They preferred to 'come back later'. We knew if we smelt vinegar anywhere except on fish and chips where it came from – on some schoolchild's hair, after the nurse had inspected it and pronounced it to be 'wick'.

What a job, I thought, being a nit nurse. I wondered how much they were paid. They must have enjoyed their career, or I don't suppose they'd have done it. Personally, I was so tense when the navy clad figure expertly flicked my hair up and down that it's a wonder I didn't have a premature heart attack. What were the right words to say if a nit was seen or caught? Did one apologise, or what? Or be grateful that the nurse hadn't, after all, been wasting her time.

One cherished memory of being in the infants' class is when we were allowed to play with the toys. There was a huge dolls' house and a big cot with a side that slid up and down – one had to beware of trapped fingers in that though when some bad little devil let the side down quickly on purpose. There was a huge one-eyed teddy bear, his other eye stuck on the end of a long piece of wire, which we could pull in and out at will. There was the biggest celluloid doll I've ever seen, a baby one with a wisp of celluloid hair over one blue eye and lots of baby clothes. Some of the more domesticated mothers knitted romper suits for it and pretty lacy dresses, bonnets and matinee coats. None of us knew really whether it was a boy or girl and weren't bothered either. It went straight through to the back underneath, with no suspicion of being boy or girl. Some of the jackets and bonnets were edged with fluffy white angora and the doll had a dummy with a bright red end, which I enjoyed pushing into the mouth and making its tongue disappear.

Deighton Council school infants' class, 1930s

There was a work table and a box full of plasticine. All the colours mixed irreversibly together. Even so, it was still fun to make plasticine men and poke eyes, nose and mouth in them with used matchsticks. Somehow, the new box of plasticine bought for me to play with at home didn't hold the same attraction as that grey, mixed up mass in the cardboard box at school. Perhaps because nobody else ever wanted to play with it when I did. It seems to be a true saying, that we always want what we cannot have!

What child today would want to say multiplication tables, hands on heads – 'two two's are four, three three's are...'. Oh, what a nightmare it all was, sounding like a swarm of bees!

FOUR

'Milk O'

⬥

My dad, an astute businessman, patronised all three of the surrounding farms. 'To keep t' band in't nick' and to ensure three lots of milkmen's wives as customers.

Ephraim, of the cauliflower ear and thick, black rimmed spectacles, brought our first milk of the day – by horse and cart. A horse which invariably waited till it reached our shop front to urinate, much to dad's thinly disguised disgust. That and the aroma of freshly baked bread, hardly mixed to the best advantage. Ephraim, dour, down to earth, always wore the same nondescript flat, checked cap. One never thought of him as ever enjoying a youthful phase of life. Nor could one imagine him ever progressing into old age. He was permanently middle aged.

'Na mate', was his never varying morning greeting to mother. Again, echoing one's feelings that Ephraim, bachelor, was quite sexless, treating both men and women as the same breed.

Midday another horse and cart drew up outside the shop front. Old farmer Beaumont, pink-cheeked, white-haired, heavy white moustache and blue eyes. In soft, fawn trilby and a gingery linen smock, he preferred the personal touch and brought his milk cans round to the back door. He habitually hissed in mother's ear 'Ee, ah do fancy thee, gi' us a kiss'. Whether or not his request was ever granted I do not know, but our blue and white striped milk jugs were always full to overflowing.

Our third milkman was Mr Gawthorpe. His wife thrived on the good living her hard-working husband made possible for her, and she regularly arranged shopping excursions to the fashionable Leeds shops with mother. Mother was collected by her friend at about eight thirty to be in time for the nine o'clock train. If it was an Autumn spree, Mrs Gawthorpe wore one of her tailor-made costumes and a fox fur stole draped dressily over one angular shoulder. This 'toff' like picture was topped off by a high, turbanned hat and wrinkly, elbow length gloves.

Occasionally, the friendship between the grocer's wife and the farmer's wife was consolidated by an invitation to have tea at Meadow Farm. What teas they were! Taken in the large living room, flanked by a massive sideboard and scrubbed wooden table, the hostess served afternoon tea on a lace spread 'occasional' table. Smiling down from the high mantelpiece, two Dresden china figures of a shepherd and shepherdess lent an appropriate atmosphere to the proceedings.

Delicately cut triangles of home baked brown and white bread filled with thick, home-fed ham, followed by deep fruit basins full of whatever fruit was in season topped by lashings of cream. The piece de resistance to my mind, however, was Mrs Gawthorpe's home made gingery, crackly brandy snaps. Oozing thick whipped cream from

Hilda Taylor shopping in New Street in the 1920s with a new 78rpm record under her arm.

either end and right through the middle too. We felt when we'd eaten our fill that our bodies were made up of cream, we were urged to sample so much.

The smell of mansion polish competed with the more earthy smells which floated in through the casement windows. Mrs Gawthorpe brought out her best fluted china tea service decorated with full blown roses and edged with what mother imagined to be pure gold for these gossipy, *tête à tête* teas. Both ladies drank their tea with little fingers genteely crooked to one side – it used to be the fashion then – among those who 'knew a thing or two'. Unlike the common herd, as Mrs Gawthorpe was wont to say. Though doubtless both resorted to normal finger positioning when alone. After 'oohing' and 'aahing' about the goings on in the village, mother, timid soul, had to be escorted all the way home to the shop by farmer Gawthorpe lest a stray cow or bull formed a sudden attachment to her.

Nevertheless, mother did love all animals, the big ones at arm's length. Regularly each morning she leant over the fence which separated our back garden from one of Mr Beaumont's fields and brought three of his cows hurtling to her by gently cooing her pet names for them; Beauty, Sulky and Buttercup. One night, however, the trio visited the back garden uninvited. Someone had foolishly left the garden gate open and mother had left a washing line out full of newly washed stockings. Next morning, they had all disappeared – except for a few chewed remains still pegged to the line. Beauty, Sulky and Buttercup were not as eager as usual for the previous day's leftover loaves which were thrown out for them. Whether or not the stockings affected the quality of the ensuing milk no-one knows, but I hardly remember it coming out a light beige shade. It didn't worry mother much. There were plenty more boxes of artificial silk stockings on the shop shelves, at only 1/11½d a pair. Her economics told her that, living at the shop as she did, they didn't actually have to be bought.

We had quite a shock another night. The door knob rattled urgently and we wondered it was some parent wanting a bottle of fever cure or a Gregory powder for a fretful child. Mother opened the door and a huge wet nose thrust itself at her terrified figure. It was old Ben, the cart horse that lived in the field with the three cows when he was off duty. Obviously he desired a change of company and was equally determined to have it!

FIVE

Free Gifts

⤨

No matter what the era, no-one can resist the lure of 'free gifts' – even though they may really have been paid for in an obscure way beforehand. As a child in the early thirties, one of my greatest delights was looking through a catalogue of gifts obtainable in exchange for soap wrappers. The soap was Goodwin's 'Ivy' brand. An elderly aunt recalled that Ivy soap was a godsend in the bath as it never became lost – it floated on the water.

Besides illustrations of gifts for the home, there were also lots of 'hints'. Hints on the care of furniture, home furnishing and hints on the care of clothes. What lady in those days could get through a week without needlework hints and economy hints? There were miscellaneous hints and nursery hints ('The nursery – the hallowed birthplace of domestic joy') – passing some of our customer's homes and hearing the bellowing infants there suggested that this description was debatable.

In the absence of a National Health Service, families could not afford to call in a doctor willy-nilly so there were plenty of home remedy hints and poultice hints, as well as washing and ironing hints. People were very fond of tips in those days. Tips on the use of lemons, baking cakes and so on, anything to save a few coppers.

But to return to the great decision! What were we to get for our precious bundle of wrappers, held together with a thick rubber band from a sardine jar and kept safe in the sideboard drawer? The big debate took place round the kitchen table. We checked and re-checked the number of wrappers. We made up our minds and then changed them again. My inclination was for a toy or game; I could be the proud owner of a mouth organ for only twenty-four labels, or look forward to the postman bringing a bright new box of paints for

Nursery Hints

" The nursery—the hallowed birthplace of domestic joy."

THOUGH Mother Shipton died childless, and was without nursery experience, the association of her name with Goodwin's time-honoured Annual Distribution of Free Christmas Toys has enthroned her personality in the hearts of children, thousands of whom, in addition to the pleasure afforded by the toys, owe a large measure of their general welfare and happiness to the improved conditions that prevail at home, when " Mother Shipton's " Soap is regularly used for laundry and household purposes.

We believe our readers will discern in Mother Shipton's Nursery Hints the same vein of homely common sense as runs through the other items of domestic information appearing throughout the book.

Accustom children to sleep without a light.

Bottle foods should be freshly made for each meal.

Never use Soda in the washing of baby's clothes.

Dry, cold fresh air cannot harm a warmly clad child.

If baby's scalp becomes scaly, rub a little olive oil gently into it.

Whooping cough invariably calls for prompt medical treatment.

Treat measles as a dangerous disease, as its after-effects often prove it to be.

Children's night attire should consist of woollen sleeping suits, as these afford protection against cold when bed clothes are kicked off.

Constipation in infants can be remedied by adding cream to the food, or by giving frequent small doses of castor oil. As the child grows, try baked apples and cream or the juice of stewed prunes.

Croup.—Get medical advice at earliest possible moment. Meanwhile put the child into a hot bath, or dash hot and cold water over it alternately. Administer a teaspoonful of ipecacuanha wine, and put finger down the child's throat to excite vomiting.

'Hints' from the wrappers catalogue, 1930s.

the same number. How about the pyramid blocks, a table game, stencil set, or a box of modelling wax, but then, how about the large rubber ball? A printing outfit would be lovely, or even a school set consisting of ruler, compass, rubber and other scholastic necessities, neatly held together in a folding case.

It was a cosy way of spending an evening. The big fire burning brightly in the Yorkshire range, the shop bell tinkling as customers trailed in and out till closing time. Dad reading the 'local rag' and smoking his fags in between serving. Then the drawing down of the shop blinds and the snuggly, closed in, secure feeling of being just we four altogether in the back kitchen. Not forgetting the array of cats, of course, and Prince the dog.

Besides illustrations of Gifts For The Home, there were lots of household hints in the catalogue to save wear and tear. With a big, part sheepdog part collie, sprawled in one armchair and cats dotted about on the others, one could hardly say we lived up to one of these hints – 'the greater the care, the longer the wear'.

Brother Philip and I were detailed to count the wrappers first, then to pass them over to mother for checking. Oh, the times we made up our minds, flicked over and changed them again. 'There's enough for a football' suggested Philip, 'but the mouth organ's only twenty four labels', I objected, 'Or we can share a box of paints for the same number'.

'Let's have a decco,' dad would say, grabbing the cata-logue, 'let the dog see the rab-

Trixie the shop cat in the garden, 1920s.

Opposite & overleaf: *A selection of 'gifts' from the wrappers catalogue, 1930s.*

32

Coloured Alarm Clock.
120 Wrappers.

Fibre
Lunch Case.
96 Wrappers.

Boy's Watch.
120 Wrappers.

Schoolbag.
.96 Wrappers.

Oak Clock.   240 Wrappers.

Box Camera.
2¼″×3¼″ Film.
240 Wrappers.

Child's
Umbrella.
72 Wrappers.

Fountain Pen.
96 Wrappers.

Wash Leather.
72 Wrappers.

Photo Snap
Album.
48 Wrappers.

Camera Case.
2¼″×3¼″.   96 Wrappers.

Tea Cosy.
72 Wrappers.

Writing Case.
72 Wrappers.

Brush and
Crumb Tray.
120 Wrappers.

33

Aluminium Porringer
96 Wrappers.

Family Scales.
180 Wrappers.

Aluminium
Coffee Pot.
96 Wrappers.

Aluminium Kettle.
4 Pint.
120 Wrappers.

Aluminium
Fit-All Steamer.
72 Wrappers.

Aluminium Teapot.
120 Wrappers.

Aluminium
3-Taper Saucepans.
96 Wrappers

Aluminium
Egg Poacher.
60 Wrappers.

Aluminium
Frying Pan.
60 Wrappers.

Mincing Machine.
5 Cutters. 180 Wrappers.

Aluminium
Chip Pan.
96 Wrappers.

34

bit'. 'Now then, never mind the toys, the place is overflowing with them, what about a cocoa house broom for forty-eight wrappers or a whisk carpet brush. How about a pair of 'ladies artificial silk hose, in mushroom, gun metal, grey, beige, squirrel, omar, or new brown' to go with the hundreds and thousands you've got in your bedroom Mama, he teased our mother.

'Pooh', sniffed mother derisively, 'there's an ebonised hand mirror here for ninety-six wrappers – have we got that many? Or shall we settle for a few small gifts, instead of using all the coupons on one? Oh, how to make one's mind up!

Perhaps dad might like a gents' artificial silk tie, or a razor strop, new braces or a nickel cigarette case? I used to think men looked ever so sophisticated when they nonchalantly flicked open those slim shiny cases. Then again, how about a jazzily striped, artificial silk scarf instead? Goodwin's Myrtle shaving sticks were only eighteen wrappers or per- haps dad could get a pair of men's suspenders to hold his socks up!

'I'd like a new watch,' remarked Philip. But I'd like a box camera too.' 'We could use the fibre lunch case for taking picnics in', said mother beginning to yawn.

'To save jealousy, let's send off for something for the house, so we can all benefit from the coupons,' decided dad, seeing that the whole evening was in danger of being wasted if a decision wasn't arrived at soon.

'Goodness, 240 wrappers for a handsome oak clock to stand in the middle of the mantelpiece! What about unwrapping a lot of soap eh?' 'On the other hand we could have a Jaspe bedspread or an Alhambra bed quilt', concluded mother, getting up to make a drink. We kept on turning the pages backwards and forwards, it was like a drug that we couldn't put down. There were EPNS knives and forks, serviette rings, sugar sifters, sugar tongs, butter knives, fish servers. Aluminium goods were popular at the time so there were porringers, teapots, egg poach- ers, steamers and frying pans to save for as well. Lots and lots of differ- ent types of brushes: banister brushes, hall brush sets with a mirror insert, paint brushes, scrubbing brushes. Come to think of it, nobody ever seems to brush their clothes nowadays – it used to be as normal a thing as brushing one's teeth, giving a flick with the clothes brush before going out.

Whatever gift was eventually selected, there was an air of great expectancy about the house from the minute we carefully wrapped up the required number of labels and sent them off. We parcelled them up in brown paper, stuck the edges down with sealing wax and tied them up with lots of string then printed our address, 'Central Stores', in big block capital letters inside the parcel. Then to bed to look forward, in the hopefully near future, to the uniformed postman coming tinkling in at the shop door with our gift.

I wonder how much that tatty old catalogue itself would fetch today if displayed in a flea market?

SIX

The Sunday School Christmas Party

~≈~

Children missed a lot if they don't go to Sunday School, quite apart from the religious aspect. When I was a child in the thirties, the highlight of my year was the Sunday School Christmas party. We were asked to take some food (with our parents' permission) before it actually began. Some children offered to contribute jellies, others cakes, some sandwiches. The latter were never what could be termed 'posh'. But they were very moreish! Thinly cut bread and butter, I doubt if there was sliced bread then, spread liberally with Shippams' bloater or anchovy paste, and little pots of mustard dotted along the tables. How those long tables inspired awe in me, covered with stiffly starched cloths. The prospect of eating with such a lot of people all at once was very exciting.

My brother Philip and I took lots of food, living at the village shop and we could choose what we liked. Iced buns in wrinkly paper cases, some with white icing on top, some with a quarter of a glace cherry, coconut, or bright pink icing.

Father Christmas had promised to visit our Sunday School party and my heart thumped with anticipation all day. My excitement was heightened by the annual liberty bodice argument beforehand. It was such a novelty to be allowed to wear a thin party dress in late December but then my mother ruined it all by insisting that I wear a thick, fleecy lined liberty bodice underneath. She said I'd catch pneumonia if I didn't. I think I'd have preferred pneumonia than having the glamour snatched away. So mother put it on, I tore it off. After a few repetitions it was finally buttoned firmly down the middle and always ended up cossetting

my flat torso beneath my party dress. I recall one pink satin dress in particular when I was five years old. The skirt was made up of five deep frills
and dainty cape sleeves framed my upper arms. I loved the sensuous
slither of them as I moved.

The party for the primary school scholars began about four o'clock.
As mother walked hand in hand with us down the hill, the wintry sun
had already disappeared and I was secretly thankful for the warmth of the
liberty bodice and fluffy angora cardigan over my dress. In those days I
wore buttoned up garters over my legs and a tweed overcoat with a velvet stitched collar. Everything looked so festive in the big main hall of the
school. Coloured streamers, paper Chinese lanterns and scores of
brightly coloured balloons swaying from the rafters. But to me, the *pièce
de resistance* was the huge fir tree welcoming the children just inside the
doorway with tiny glass toys, entrancing baubles and little candles flickering enchantingly. If we stood near enough we could see our faces in the
bigger baubles. Silly faces, with big cheeks and flat noses. On and around
the base of the tree were presents. Pink tissue wrapped for girls, blue for
boys. At the top of the tree was the glorious silver and apparently unat-
tainable fairy with her magic wand. I'd always yearned for one of those
long slim cardboard boxes with a tinsel clad fairy doll inside on
Christmas morning. I was sure her wand could grant my every wish.

The tables were already set for tea when we arrived. Lady members of
the chapel thoroughly enjoyed helping with these annual events. Thick
white Sunday school cups and saucers and plain white plates were set out
at intervals. We took our own cutlery, tied with coloured cotton, and our
names printed on a bit of paper to save washing up. As each child handed
over its offerings, helpers set them out on tiered cake stands, making sure
that each table had equal amounts of sandwiches, cakes, jellies and trifles.
It mattered little how long they were exposed in cold December, there
were no flies. The only hazard being the odd grubby, over eager outstretched paw and the occasional heavy breather hovering in glad anticipation over the feast. Some of the children had no dinner on the day of
the party. Their mothers rightly thinking they'd get a bigger 'bellyfull' at
tea-time, free, if they abstained at midday.

It was quite a procedure getting outdoor clothes off, especially if it had
been snowing or raining. Everyone walked in those days. I didn't even
know anyone who had a car. Stiff, wet wellingtons were terrible to
wrench off. I had to prise myself against a wall and stick one leg out while

mother bent double and yanked, it's a wonder my whole leg didn't come off. Once she pulled so hard the wellington shot out of her hand and hit one of the helpers in the face, while I landed up on the wooden floor-boards, dazed. The hard forms we sat on ran all round the room and they were attached to the walls. In the two smaller classrooms adjoining were tiny chairs, which were brought into the hall if extra seating was required.

My long black woollen socks were exchanged for a new pair of white ankle socks and how the other little girls admired my silver dancing slip-pers! They had flat, fluffy pom-poms on the front and I thought I resem-bled Shirley Temple. Especially as my hair had been bound up in rags all afternoon. I hardly dare put my feet down lest some of the rougher ele-ments, 'big' boys of seven or eight who had only heavy boots to wear, lunged onto them in a wild fever of Christmas clumsiness.

Big boys weren't the only hazard after my mother had left, with prom-ises that she would be back to take us home again when the party was over. Little girls who's parents couldn't afford real party dresses for them

Philip Taylor dressed for Sunday school but trying out Uncle Kenneth's motorbike before setting off.

(soap either, by the look of their fingernails!) were dazzled by new dresses on others. Their envy made me feel slightly embarrassed. As they nuzzled near, grimy fingers lifted satin frills, pawing the soft material while I stood frozen with apprehension. 'Aw, in't it luvvly? D'you fink yer muvver'll let us 'ave it when you've done wi' it, eh?' I said nothing, for I hoped that by summertime I'd be able to swank with it at weekday school, not keep it solely for Sundays. Then there was no such thing as buying clothes specially for casual wear, we just wore last year's best.

When we were all seated, a teacher said Grace, 'For what we are about to receive may the Lord make us truly thankful'.

Then everyone began chattering as helpers poured tea from the massive urn stationed at the top of the tables. Some of the children only ate the insides of the sandwiches, leaving the crusts on their plates, or hid them beneath their next door neighbour's saucer. If one of our austere Sunday School teachers spied such a happening a sharp look was enough and the crusts were retrieved and quickly downed. I always felt self-conscious seeing grandad's iced buns on the table and never ate any. It was more interesting, if dangerous, to eat other people's concoctions. They looked highly coloured and slightly evil and some mothers had spread margarine on the sandwiches. We never had that at home – at the shop it was always butter.

There was always one infant who had to forego the pleasures of the table and be hastily ushered into the cloakroom to be sick. After waiting all year for the big event, the actuality proved too much. When this happened the rest of us round the table went deadly quiet, straining our ears to listen to the terrible retchings, which served as accompaniment to the carols being thumped out on the piano by the Sunday School Superintendent. After tea there were lots of games, made all the better by having loads of floor space to play them on.

The late lamented Joyce Grenfell could have moulded her act on one of our teachers. Over enthusiastically she called out, 'Now, all make a big, big, circle for King William...' This was my first experience of the stirrings of youthful attractions! How silly and conspicuous I felt, stumbling round in a circle wondering if Jim, the farmer's son, who had such lovely red cheeks and bright blue eyes and was in the centre of the ring, would choose me. From out the East or West. 'Down on this carpet you shall kneel, while the grass grows round your feet...' What a leper, what an outcast we felt to be if we weren't choseen quite early on in the proceedings!

Most times however, the lads, lest they be called cissies, grabbed another boy, amid loud boos from the little girls. While even if a girl was King William she usually chose her best friend, probably denying her own heart. So, although it did have its moments of excitement, it was a washout really. I preferred Postman's Knock or Cat and Mouse. For this, tension rose to fever pitch. A huge circle of infants, elbows stuck out in all directions to stop the 'cat' from catching the 'mouse' while screams soared to the rooftops. Oh what near escapes! Oh the ribbons, sashes, or boys ties that were almost snatched by the darting cat!

Lucy Lockett was another favourite, but how I wished that cushions were provided. Those bare wooden floorboards were ever so hard and frequently full of splinters too. 'Is my dress dirty' was the girls' main anxiety as the, 'Drop it, drop it,' droned on interminably. I doubt that many children will even possess a handkerchief today, they'll all have rainbow coloured tissues instead.

Throughout all the activities, one central thought remained paramount in my mind, Father Christmas was actually going to come to our Sunday School that very evening! Hearts thumped with wild expectation as we grouped round the piano to sing carols. 'He' usually appeared, whiskery head thrust round the doorway, sometimes during this lull in the boisterous games. 'Good King Wencleslas' was the favourite and everybody wanted to be King or Page so they could sing solos and feel important. Runners up were 'While Shepherd Watched their Flocks by Night' (some of the lads 'washed their socks by night'), 'Away in a Manger,' and 'I saw Three Ships go Sailing by'.

Frequently a hand faltered into the air and a small voice enquired 'Please Miss, is he coming yet?' At last, there was a huge knocking at the door and a deep gruff voice calling 'Merry Christmas, one and all, may I come in?' I felt half mad with delight, yet at the same time a bit frightened. Teacher selected a child to go and open the door, with instructions to say 'Welcome Father Christmas'. Then, in staggered a bent figure in red cloak, long, white wavy beard, thick wavy white hair and drooping moustache. Cheeks ruddy, eyes twinkling, always blue, never brown.

'Hello children, hello', he hailed. Many rushed toward the genial figure, shouting and yelling, trying to catch one of his hands but others were twisting fingers in their dresses, dissolving into tears or hiding behind the teacher's skirt.

First the old man joined in a carol round the piano and then ate a mince pie and piece of cheese, with a drop of Communion wine to wash it down. Being Methodists, alcoholic drinks were strictly forbidden. Then he dragged the huge sack into the centre of the hall, sat on the floor cross-legged and dived a gnarled old hand into the depths of the sack. Presents were pulled out, names called.

Little girls accepted shyly and blushed deeply when Santa Claus hugged them and planted a kiss on their cheeks. Big boys shouted 'Worav yer got?' to chums and 'Can I have a Meccano set on Christmas Eve Mister?' or other much desired game or toy of the era. But for the present, painting books, boxes of water colour paints, packets of crayons, tiny celluloid baby dolls with 'dum tits' hanging on a string round their necks, books of dressing dolls and miniature cars were handed out. How I envied those who's mothers could knit pretty clothes for their baby dolls – woollen 'pull ups', matinee jackets and angora trimmed bonnets. Mine never could. So she wrapped my dolls in scraps of velvet or other remnant and held the shawl together with a big safety pin.

What pure happiness those Sunday School Christmas parties were. When the sack lay limp on the floor and every scholar had received a present, Father Christmas took one of the youngest children on his knees for a farewell carol. Everyone shoved and pushed to get nearer to the magic presence. None of us ever realised that the ethereal character was one we saw every Sunday morning in chapel!

When parents drifted in to collect their children, at about half past six, boys lined up on one side of the tree, girls on the other and all were handed an orange, a new silver threepenny piece, an apple and a silver-wrapped tangerine before going out into the frosty air. Ah yes, having to wear the liberty bodice at a Sunday School party and exchanging my silver slippers for Wellingtons to walk home, never took away the sheer thrill of those annual festivities at our Sunday School Christmas party.

SEVEN

Huddersfield's Ideal Home Exhibition

Ideal Home Exhibitions have long been popular. In 1935 the third Huddersfield Health Week and Health and Traders' Exhibition was housed in the Drill Hall with additional exhibits in the Temperance Hall. Health was the main factor of the exhibition and it was supported by the Huddersfield Health Department.

Madame Leene, London's premier palmist, was an additional draw to the public. Displays were given by the Women's League of Health and Beauty, whose local address was St Patrick's Hall. At that time tap dancing was all the rage and members gave displays. Exhibitors and representatives were not allowed to solicit orders except at their own stands. Visitors were requested to report (in confidence) any instance of 'undue pressure'. Electrical work was carried out by Messrs G. Garton & Sons Ltd of Market Place.

Among the list of standholders was Whitfields Ltd, of Ramsden Street. Shoppers thought it wonderful when in later years after browsing among the furniture, a coffee bar was installed upstairs and they could halt for refreshment without having to go into a 'proper' cafe.

Other familiar Huddersfield trade names were John Mollett & Co, John William Street, Thornton & Ross, Milnsbridge and Huddersfield Corporation Electricity Department. Tennant and Rotherford of Queen Street, J. Holroyd & Co, Huddersfield Sanitary Laundry and Newtown Laundry. Parcelling up the washing for the laundryman to take away was the housewife's idea of saving precious time.

On stand 56 was ice-cream maker D. Coletta of 39 Westgate. (Oh, those delicious, unbeatable ice cream cornets of the thirties! They were superior

St Georges Square, Huddersfield, c. 1910.

to any other more famous names, I always thought.) Sitting in the tin bath, brought up from the cellar and filled with water on the lawn, on a sunny day during the school holidays and sucking on a Coletta's cornet was my idea of heaven!

Huddersfield's then Medical Officer of Health, Dr John M. Gibson, Chief School Medical Officer, wrote in the booklet printed to commemorate the event, how, in ancient times, everything relating to health was closely associated with superstition. Lucky charms were believed to be much more efficacious in safeguarding health than any agency under human control. 'There never was a time in the world's history when so much was performed at the public expense to provide health and combat disease' he wrote. 'Much more can yet be done if the public will take advantage of the facilities offered and services provided.'

Many children during the thirties succumbed to diptheria. I well remember the carry-on that ensued when, receiving a communication about vaccination against the disease, signed by Dr John M. Gibson, my mother refused to allow my brother and I to have 'that poison' put into our bodies. Fortunately we never suffered from diptheria, despite not taking advantage of the offer to be vaccinated.

As far back as 1935 smokeless fuel was advocated and what ages must elapse before mankind pays heed to the truths about health as stated even then. Sir Arbuthnot Lane, who opened the Huddersfield exhibition said, 'if money annually contributed to the upkeep of hospitals, asylums and gaols were devoted to the education of the public in health matters, there would be no necessity for these institutions.' He also commented on those with 'warped minds' who could think of nothing but £sd and said 'we are digging graves with out teeth'.

The adverts are so different to those of today. When only the well-to-do had central heating, ordinary householders were advised to use 'Odelus' firelighters. Available in packets of seven for 3½d. 'Odelus earns the thanks of all good men folk – no firewood to chop at the weekend.'

A furnished show house on the Maplin Leas Estate, off Carr Street, Marsh, was on view each day and weekends. Prices for such a house were £420, repayments 10/6 per week and Mr R. Smith of Luck Lane was the builder. That well-known builder J. Wimpenny, of Spurn Point, Linthwaite, was selling houses and bungalows from £390, while Isaac Timmins were building on Greenhead Estate, Dalton, at prices from £395 upwards.

In that year George Hall had an outfitting shop at 20 King Street. During 'Health Week' they had special displays of ladies' and children's all wool underwear. George Hall's was THE place to go for Greenhead High School uniforms too. Customers could also buy Cash's name tapes, prior to that arduous task of stitching the tags onto every school garment. While tweed coats kept at bay

A typical Huddersfield back yard photographed off King Street in 1983 but largely unchanged since the 1930s.

autumn chills from the outside, plentiful meals of tripe and onions were supposed to keep health at peak form on the inside. J.S. Gibson, of 18 Beast Market sold tons of the stuff in the thirties.

Fresh air and open windows while sleeping were recommended if the air was pure, but in the then smoky atmosphere from mill chimneys and with everybody puffing on cigarettes and burning coal, the public were advised in the Health Week Booklet to 'use a cheese cloth screen beneath the lower sash of the window to filter out the soot and dust'.

The programme carried many advertisements for local firms. Those who required spectacles in those days will recall optician Mr A. Archard, whose premises were in the Old Upper Market Hall. J.E. Wood, Son and Co. had the 'Big Fish Shop', Victoria Lane and 34 Westgate at the time of this exhibition. While Gilbert Vizard (established 1897) manufactured the Thomas hip and knee splints, artificial limbs, surgical boots, trusses (with and without springs) orthopaedic appliances, where lady and gentleman fitters could be consulted at their premises at 20 Queen Street. Or if chimney pots were the problem, they could be fixed by Walter Riley, plasterer, of Paddock.

Also advertising in the pamphlet were Calam's Bread and Confectionery, of Royd Bakery, Ash Brow, Sheepridge. My Saturday teatime treat used to be one of their cream cake specialities. How to choose between a delicious jam and cream filled puff pastry horn, chocolate covered eclair, a huge 'waff and fuff' concoction spilling over with cream, or a delectable meringue with chocolate encasing the twirls of cream....! What heaven to be young in 1935, when a cream cake was something to covet, not to be warned against! Ovaltine, however, advertised as 'The Supreme Beverage of Health' and sold in tins at 1/1d, 1/10d and 3/3d used to make me feel sick simply by looking at it. Even so, I followed the herd and became an 'Ovaltinie' in order to get the badge and enjoy the feeling of being one of the 'we are the Ovaltinies, Little Girls and Boys' as the song went.

I seem to have eaten lots of cream cakes but haven't come to much harm yet, in fact I've always subscribed to the maxim that 'a little of what you fancy does you good!'

EIGHT

Married Ladies' Concerts

How I loved those married ladies' concerts of the thirties! Mother was one of the star turns, she could always be relied upon to have the audience rolling with laughter as they sat on their hard wooden forms in the Sunday school-cum-concert hall.

Once, when made up as a man, because she was the tallest and flattest married lady they had, mother appeared, after an involved tussle with the tatty red plush curtains, with black, twirly moustache vertically against her left cheek instead of horizontally across her upper lip. Another time she swaggered on stage immaculate in top hat and tails and swinging a silver topped cane, confident that this time she was correct in every detail. A raucous Yorkshire voice jeered, 'Shows she's not used to trousers, t'buttons aren't done up'

In contrast to the grocer's wife, the coalman's wife never, ever put a foot wrong. Every October or thereabouts, out came her 'prima donna' dress of long black lace, while the inevitable white carnation graced her throbbing white bosom. Long white evening gloves failed to conceal her plump, dimpling elbows. As the strains of 'Velia' rang out, the coalman's wife glided to the centre of the stage, pink with pleasure. Her flimsy handkerchief, never meant for use, fluttered gracefully from natural Amami-buffed fingertips. Nut brown hair, parted neatly down the centre with ever-so-stiff marcelled waves, crinkling on each side and ending in a row of tight curls, reminding me of eight shiny sausage rolls, without the grease. After the preliminary ripple of applause, the audience greeted the coalman's wife with the respectful silence she felt to be her due. Blue eyes seemed to roll upwards to the rafters of the old school roof, where the odd sparrow often lent an uninvited accompaniment; white gloved hands were clasped and unclasped a score of times before the black lace sank to

A Married Ladies' Concert at Deighton Sunday School in the late 1920s. Hazel's mother, Hilda, is in the back row on the left with a drum.

the floor in a deep curtsy to her husband's loyal customers and the plump satisfied face was momentarily hidden by the crown of the nut-brown head, thus marking the end of dear Velia for yet another year.

After such concentration and culture it was something of an unspoken relief for many when a comic act or sketch was announced. Here was ripe opportunity for the wits in the audience.

Ladies taking part in the sketches had to put in as many as four nights rehearsal a week during the last hectic days before opening night. But they were never word perfect. Which was a blessing, as lapses of memory helped the fun along. Those awkward silences and hot flushes on the night were probably brought about not by lack of rehearsal, but because a host of critical relations and acquaintances were there out front.

There was added cachet for those in the audience who had lent props for the sketches. They weren't going to let their generosity go unnoticed. 'See that chair, it's ours. Its from our kitchen.' The information was imparted to all and sundry in much more than a stage whisper, no wonder the would-be Ellen Terrys on stage were occasionally flummoxed.

Ladies too modest to cavort on stage, enjoyed the months of sewing colourful costumes. They felt a great sense of importance should there be a button to stitch on or a tear to mend immediately before an importance entrance. Perhaps their greatest reward came when the whole cast gathered together for numbers such as 'Oh, play to me Gypsy', or similar hit tunes of the day, and the audience oohed and aahed, and exclaimed delight, at the colourful array of gypsy raiment.

Down in the darkened auditorium I, as a child of ten or eleven, felt the first twinges of romantic yearnings. I vowed to myself that when I grew up I'd marry a gypsy, a dark and swarthy man who played a violin from morn till night and we'd have a colony of black cats and a rough haired dog call Gyp and when we invited mother and dad to tea in our caravan we'd have dandelion leaves for salad, but draw the line at hedgehogs baked in clay.

I attended those concerts on Wednesday, Thursday and Friday nights just for the gypsy songs. It was sad when Saturday came, and the last night. Then the school was packed. Most of the ladies invited friends and relations to tea prior to the grand finale. On one such occasion, a certain tubby lady stole the show quite unwittingly. Mrs Muffit had the wrong pair of cricket flannels on by mistake and they were much, much too tight – skin tight. As she appeared mid-stage following the other lady cricketers her little bow legs clad in the too tight cricket flannels created complete uproar. Little did she realise what a profile she cut, with her uncorseted tummy protruding above!

A Married Ladies Concert at Deighton in around 1933. Hazel's mother is in the middle dressed as a man.

It was too much for her husband. He had to be helped out of the Sunday school, tears rolling down his cheeks, hysterical with laughter.

Alas, times have changed. The young married ladies of today are too busy attending evening classes in autumn and winter, learning to speak foreign languages for next year's holiday abroad, learning yoga or cooking exotic dishes before lolling before the TV set to watch professionals who never forget their lines. But they will never know the thrill, that magic moment, of 'curtain up' which we knew, who made up the audiences of their predecessors. Curtain up for the grocer's wife, the coalman's, the fish and chip shop proprietor's 'missus' and just about every village married lady there was.

For me, anyway, no sophisticated play on television can ever recapture those laughter-filled evenings in autumn, when Married Ladies' Concerts were the highlights of our village life.

NINE

The Artist's Cottage

⟨⟩

It was a lovely walk up to 'Owd Trulove's' cottage at the top of Shockey Lane. One we never tired of. The way lay up a long, winding path between hawthorn hedges and wide green fields where horses grazed in summertime. Fields full of clover and buttercups and daisies. Where we paused to make daisy chains and hang them round our necks and pretend we were Queens or Fairies. Fat brown and white cows stared and mooed at us as they peered over the hedges, chewing lazily. Bees buzzed happily, a farm cat basked in the sunshine, a sense of peace encompassed the place be it summer or winter. An ideal setting for an artist.

'Owd Truelove, as he was known in the village, was what is commonly known as a knackler. A chap who made his living by doing odd jobs, in his own time. Mending a garden gate, or a garden fence, selling a few freshly laid eggs to passers-by. There was always a chalked sign on a bit of wood outside his stone cottage, advertising his wares. Sometimes he earned a few coppers by taking his ferrets to sort out a few rats for somebody. Most of all, he had an artist's eye for nature and was supremely content with his lot, humble though it probably seemed to some eyes.

His cottage, round, stone and weather beaten, had a wonderful hotch potch of nick-knacks inside. I was always entranced with a stuffed fox in a glass case – caught and stuffed by the old man, of course, but even more so by another, larger case on the antique sideboard. Inside were miniature figures of gypsies, tiny caravans, a couple of horses and an exquisitely fashioned dog. All carved with a penknife by Herbert Truelove, then painted. They were grouped round what first appeared to be a blazing fire, but on further scrutiny was revealed to be red crinkly crepe paper stuffed convincingly into a black container. So life-like was the scene that I really wouldn't have been surprised if one of the gypsies had sprung up and tried to sell me some of her tiny pegs.

Herbert 'Owd Truelove' with his dog in the garden.

'Owd Truelove' told dad and me one afternoon, 'Everything in that case ah carved mesen wi' bits of old wood and me old penknife. Twenty year sin', a chap offered me twenty pounds, nay, he went to fifty, if ah'd nobbut sell it to him. But no, ah wouldn't part wi' it for owt. Ah made it for my missus, and hers it'll stay, gone though she is.'

Going for a stroll up the Shockey, to see 'Owd Truelove', was a favourite way of passing Wednesday afternoons, half day closing. He was such a relaxing character to be with. Unconcerned with superficial appearances, he took you as you were, and expected one to do the same with him.

In his later years he became extremely deaf. Then visitors had to shout, and he would make a hearing aid for himself by cupping his gnarled hand over his worst ear. His neck was hollow and scrawny and never without a red and white knotted handkerchief tied round. His cheeks were permanently sucked in, in fact, he wore a permanently sucked in appearance. Almost thin enough to wriggle down a rabbit hole himself, he kept a couple of ferrets to do it for him. Bright blue eyes twinkled non-stop, as though laughing at some secret joke that never ended. Maybe it wasn't a joke at all, just sheer, down-to-earth joy of living and joy in nature.

'Come and have a look in't garden,' we were invited on lovely afternoons. 'Bring a basket and tha can tek a few raspberries home with thee.' The wild, practically untamed cottage garden was a delight. It had a narrow, crazy paving path that lost itself somewhere on the way from the ferrets' hutches to the tumbledown 'Summer house' right at the far end. I could have gone on picking raspberries for ever. It seemed too as though no matter how many we gathered, there was always as many waiting for our attention. Rip, Truelove's shaggy sheepdog and constant companion, slavered along at our heels.

Besides the free raspberries, fat green peas and eggs, the old man yanked upteem flowers up for me. How delicious everything smelt! No wonder their owner had declined a place at the Royal College of Art many years ago. With a 'what would I be doing i' London eh? Nay, it wouldn't suit me at all.' He blended into his own peculiar Yorkshire landscape too well. He was a wise man. Not striving after the moon when he had everything he wanted right where he was.

He had two grown up daughters at the time I remember him, Edith and Ada. They worked in one of the local mills and looked after 'father' as they primly called him. Apart from that, and their regular weekly visit to Central Stores for groceries, they didn't do much. Well, not as some folk would call doing much nowadays. They gardened, made patchwork quilts, knitted, sewed, mended their clothes, darned their father's socks and it was sufficient to keep them happy. Ada had another interest, she was an ardent Salvation Army officer.

It must have been a long haul all the way up the road from our shop then up the long, winding steep lane to the cottage. But there was no hurry. There was nowhere they wished to go after tea, and they had 'The Good Book' to read or they may decide to watch father painting a picture for someone. They did have one particular highlight in their lives however. When mother whispered to them, or beckoned from the kitchen doorway, 'Can you

Ada Truelove, who worked at Walter Berry's mill, in the garden at the Artist's Cottage.

53

come through a minute Misses Truelove?' The ladies weren't keen on venturing into town when they needed new clothes, so mother had an outlet in them for disposing of clothes she'd tired of. She never wore any out, she was fed up of them long before that. And they knew that Mrs Taylor always bought best quality clothes. She could get them at wholesale prices which saved a lot if she patronised the big warehouses in town that our shop dealt with. One of mother's favourite happy hunting grounds on half day closing was a couple of hours running up bills in these shops. At one time she had a different coloured umbrella for every outfit and dad played hell and threatened not to pay for them!

So when mother gave them clothes she'd tired of but which remained top quality, they were highly delighted. 'It saves the trail,' they said. Whereas most women love going round shops they couldn't bear it. However, they were too modest to take their clothes off and try them on in the back kitchen, but assured mother they were all 'splendid! splendid!' and it was 'so kind.' The following week they would be wearing their new dresses, costumes, coats or hats and blushed self-consciously as they entered the shop.

Having been 'good' to the ladies before clothing coupons and rationing were even thought of, the Misses Truelove turned out to be invaluable to mother in wartime. It was their time to do her a favour. They slyly gave her most, if not all, of their clothing coupons. Their father's too came our way as he was even less interested in fashion than they were.

'Yar Rip wouldn't know me if ah gorranother suit' he grinned impishly. As he usually had a ferret or two pushed into his coat pockets as he went about, what on earth would he do with a Saville Row suit? His own had been a good 'un to begin with, and would see him his lifetime out. Herbert preferred to be comfortable to being 'all togged up t' nines'. Every Monday morning he was the first customer, Rip at his heels, ferrets peeping from his pockets, with an old sack over his shoulder. He had it filled with leftover loaves and teacakes from Saturday. To feed his hens and other lifestock.

'How mich Joe lad' he'd enquire when the sack was bulging at the seams. 'Give us a tanner Herbert lad,' replied dad and the weekly financial transaction was completed once more.

Dad admired the hen huts 'Owd Truelove' made for his hens so much that Herbert offered to make one for our hens. How to transport it was the question. When made, Herbert enlisted the assistance of one of his daughters, Ada. He hoisted the hut onto his back, said a prayer, asking the Lord to assist him on his journey. Then he set off down the old lane, between the hedges and fields, Ada by his side to help if the hut slithered too much to one side. At long last, Central Stores came into view. Not the shop front but the back garden and hen yard. 'Whew!' panted Herbert, but eyes twinkling with a great sense of achievement. 'Na then Joe lad, wheer does ta want it?' Even the hens and the proud strutting cockerel looked at 'Owd Truelove,' artist, knackler, and Man of God, with an expression of wondrous admiration in their eyes.

TEN

Maggie

❦

Maggie lived alone in one of the low decker houses, blackened with time and soot from mill chimneys, only a few yards below the shop. No-one knew where she came from, or anything about her family, she was one of those people who simply 'are'. Seemingly not born in the accepted sense, more of a permanent blending into the environment, part of the surroundings and as indestructable as the age-old trees.

No-one could find out anything about her at all. Her dark brown eyes had a perpetual 'yonderley' expression, her verbal communications mere exclamations of 'ee, eh!' or 'ee, ah seh!'

Her happiness, however was undisputed. As long as she was allowed to slop around the village, in and out of neighbours' houses at will, she was content. She strove for nothing, and enjoyed to the full each day as it came. Maggie didn't yearn for smart clothes, holidays, marriage or anything. She had a couple of dark brown woollen jumpers and old check skirts for winter and plenty of pinnys to wear. Villagers turning out their wardrobe knew where to dispose of unwanted garments.

Outer wear was a shapeless but serviceable tweed coat, and a thick knitted cap. The latter served a dual purpose for Maggie as a tea cosy. Her outdoor ensemble was completed with a shabby wicker basket which was carried nonchalantly over her arm.

If her neighbours were too busy to talk, up to their elbows in soap suds on Monday mornings, or putting clothes through the mangle, there was always Tom. Tom, a captive audience as he sat, day in, day out, in his wheelchair. On fine days he loved to wheel himself to the open doorway and chat with passers-by. Bright sunshine poked shafts of light into the dark room behind him and tiny specks of dust danced up and down in the brightened gloom. In that one room for all purposes was a cumbersome mahogany sideboard, cluttered with yellowing photographs in gilt-edged frames and stacks of ancient newspapers. Tom's brother's high backed carving chair and a scrubbed wooden table with bulbous legs was the only other furniture. Maggie enjoyed scouring the window sill for Tom, and rubbing deep yellow coloured donkey stone along the edge.

'Ee, eh?' she exclaimed when it was done to her liking 'ee, eh?'

Apart from the easy companionship, Maggie rejoiced in a sense of responsibility. After all, everyone needs to feel they are of some use in the world, even the Maggies and Toms. As he was entirely dependant on her to 'run' errands for him, she was in and out of the shop dozens of times a day. Sometimes she called even when she didn't want to buy anything. 'Ah've just popped in for a bit of a natter,' she would announce, uneven browning teeth bared in a companionable grin. Maggie took no offence if it wasn't convenient. She'd pick up her basket and dawdle off again down the road, promising to come back later, 'when tha's not so busy.' Maggie's best friend in the village, apart from Tom, was Florrie. When her children were small and Florrie was working down at the mill for a few bob to help out, Maggie came in to heat up a can of soup for them at dinnertime. Later, whatever they told her about goings-on at school was accepted delightedly by a 'ee, eh!'

No-one ever saw Maggie without her woolly cap and usually a host of steel curlers hidden underneath. It was firmly planted on her head winter and summer alike. On hot days she'd occasionally be seen coatless, a flowered or spotted pinafore over a dress, but capless, never.

Her greatest delight in summertime was sitting on an old cushion on the wall, either outside our shop or on Florrie's garden wall. Arms folded, listening, wide-eyed to gossip. Never contributing actively to it, unless one can include her appreciative gasps of 'ee, ah?' at some extra spicy bits of information. A village lass finding herself 'in trouble' was world shattering news to Maggie, who's personal virginity was inviolate and likely to remain so. Indeed, one doubts if she would have known how to set about any liaison with a lad. She had some vague idea that courting couples 'did summat' in the grass and first a fattening tummy then a baby was the result. And that it was thought of as even worse than stealing, though neither party was put in prison.

Maggie had the enviable quality of stillness, being able to sit on the wall, perfectly still, perfectly content, watching the shifting patterns of sky and cloud. As relaxed as Tom's mangy old ginger cat, sprawled dreaming beneath the chestnut tree. But oh, the sheer excitement of winter evenings when friend Florrie invited Maggie in to listen to Henry Hall on the wireless! Still wearing her workday clothes, and woollen stockings, often wrinkled and twisted round her fat legs when a suspender came undone and the inevitable brown cap, Maggie was an enraptured Friday evening fixture.

Maggie could never figure out how sounds could come out of that wooden cabinet on top of Florrie's cupboard, but hers not to reason why. As long as that ''enery 'all keeps on playing we'll all go riding on a rainbow'. Sometimes, even Gracie Fields came into that humble low-decker house too. Shouting 'It's the biggest aspidistra in the world!' Then Maggie's face split into an even wider grin as she pointed at Florrie's aspidistra, in the green bowl in the middle of the chenille tablecover. Gracie's words were interspersed with a 'ee, ah!' Maggie probably thought that Gracie had somehow spied the much more modest aspidistra through a spyhole in the front of Florrie's new wireless set. She could always rely on a pot of tea and chunk of bread and jam for her supper to accompany the free entertainment and, as she already had her pinafore on, all she need do to get rid of the crumbs was fold the corners of her apron together and chuck them into the fire.

Life was all so simple, so easy. No fol-di-rols or la-di-da carryings-on to complicate matters. That could have been the reason for Maggie's unchangingly robust health. Never worrying about unnecessary things, or longing for what was beyond her reach.

However, when the low deckers were demolished in the late thirties, and their owners re-housed on impersonal council estates, Maggie disappeared from our lives.

There were occasional sightings of her ambling along the streets of town, aimlessly, still wearing the same old cap and carrying the same wicker basket. But somehow, the life-spring of Maggie had been extinguished. The light in her eyes vanished with the end of village life as she had known it.

ELEVEN

Fred Wood's Fish Shop

Some years ago a 'fish and chip tablet' was included in a Northern Exhibition. It filled me with dismay. What a horrid, clinical world we are now moving towards.

I remember Fred's 'chip hoile' as it was known in the thirties and forties. Autumn evenings, when fields were free of housing estates, gloriously blackberry hedged, everybody knew each other, nobody ever talked about 'stress', they didn't know what it was. If they experienced it, there was always someone caring within reach to get them through it. A fish and a pennorth often went a long way to do just that, in a newspaper, liberally doused with salt, pepper and vinegar.

Round about eight in the evening the appetising aroma of frying fish and chips mingled with that of early bonfires, the smell of fresh, damp earth and wild flowers. Michaelmas daisies in cottage gardens lent enchantment to the humblest home. Up the road from our shop, near enough for us to run up for fish and chips however many times needed, depending on who dropped in at meal times, then back again while they were still hot, wonderful! In those days it was a cheap, sustaining meal. The first twirls of smoke from the little building announced that 'Fred was frying tonight.' Friday dinner times were especially busy too, and I mean middle of the day, not the posh Southerner's evening meal! A naked bulb, glowing yellow, the lamp lit outside, children playing, running in and out to ask Fred 'ave yer any bits Fred?' The sounds of Henry Hall's band playing 'We'll all go Riding on a Rainbow' came from Fred's wireless set. Life was magic, revolving round the fish and chip hoile.

Fred seemed to belong, as children did in those days, to the great outdoors. Door always wide open to let out the steam, sometimes belching clouds of smoke. Sometimes Fred yelled out a warning to 'Indians' and

'Cowboys' that the pursuer was catching up on them. Or he pointed to the low stone wall at the back of his shop, adjoining farmer Beaumont's field. We knew then to lie low, the enemy was lurking nearby. Often Fred clambered over the wall at dinner time to have a few kicks if lads decided to have a game of football, during a slack period while Edith, 'the missus' looked after the frying.

Girls loved to build 'houses' in this field when playing out after school. Stones placed together in squares made 'rooms,' empty cotton reels for fairies to use as tables, colourful nasturtiams when in season pushed into jam jars for decoration. A tree trunk broken down to sit on, nipping over the wall to ask Fred 'av yer any specials to spare Fred?' was usually rewarded with a tasty load of crisp leftovers in a newspaper. Men used Fred's fish shop as a kind of club. As they did our bakehouse too a few yards from the shop. Smoking a pipe of 'baccy' having a few fags, comparing notes about Huddersfield Town's team. The 'Woolpack' pub was a few yards further up the road, handy for 'swilling down' a fish and a pennorth.

Ginger, a battered old village tom cat, with bent ears and squint eyes, loved Fred's fish shop too. Sunning himself on the 'ack' (roof) in summertime, or curled round the blackened chimney as nights drew in. After prowling the far corners of the darkening fields in the hope of catching a plump mouse to precede his fish supper. The fish shop was the centre of his life as well as the people's.

As the evenings wore on, birds sought their nests, crying and chirruping, fighting for a comfortable part of the nest, eager for rest after a long day's work.

Saturday night was 'going to the pictures' night, always the last port of call for those living in Deighton being Fred's. Those living up in Sheepridge bought their fish and chips from Tom Oddy's. Fred was quite content to hear about the film second hand. Slowly turning the fish and pennorths to a golden brown in the boiling fat, then tossing them neatly to the back of the big pan to drain off.

He desired nothing more than the shop and his pals calling in to lean over the counter and 'tell the tale.' His one night out was a game or two of billiards down at the working men's club, while a neighbour helped 'his missus' in the shop. Everybody knew Fred and he knew everybody, so did his jolly, thin and wiry, beloved wife Edith. She enjoyed being in the Married Ladies concerts down at the Sunday school in autumn. They had a son and a daughter, Dennis and Barbara. What more could a man want?

Sheepridge Road, Deighton, 1920s. On the left was Tom Oddy's fish and chips shop and further up by the trees was Dobson's boiled sweets.

Then came the devastating day when he was warned the shop had to be demolished to make way for widening the road and building a council estate. After that, nothing was the same. We lost sight of Fred and, it seemed, stopped playing out on golden autumn evenings, did our homework, grew up, married and had children of our own too. All that remains of those halcyon village years of sweet content is in the memories and old photographs of those who were there.

TWELVE

Bonfire Night & 'Yep'

B onfire day was the culmination of dark nights, dark deeds, flickering gas lamps and the autumn feud between Taylor's gang (those who 'chumped' for our bonfire held in the long back garden at the back of the shop' kitchen) and 'Yep' Lindley who lived further up the road and organised his gang's 5 November festivities on the 'rec' (recreation ground) behind the council school. Eric became 'Yep' because that was his response to everything in the manner of cowboys at the time. War was declared between Yep's gang and our shop's gang. Our lot, in those tension packed October evenings of the thirties, was led by my brother Philip, because our big garden at the back of the shop was the site of Taylor's bonfire, the best in the locality. That was so long as Yep and his gang could be successfully beaten off on their frequent night raids. It was a simple operation for the enemy to swoop down the sloping fields in between, under cover of nightfall, and cart off precious 'chumps.' So frequent did those raids become when November showed on the calendar that we hardly dared speak indoors, let alone have the wireless on, lest we miss a tell tale rustle outside. Many an hour was spent peering out of the back bedroom window on cold, wet and windy evenings when it was pleasanter to remain indoors than outside playing 'Relievo' or chumping, on guard in case Yep and his followers hove into view.

If they did appear, an almighty shout went up 'He's here!' Doors were flung open, news passed on the grapevine to Taylor's gang who might be idly listening to Henry Hall's band or Gracie Fields bawling on about her aspidistra, that invasion was imminent. Lads and lasses poured out from the little 'low decker' dwellings round about, ready for battle. Prince the dog joined enthusiastically into the fray, barking vociferously at the shadowy figures nearing the boundary fence. Homework suffered when minds were more on the protection of our precious chumps, piled high like a wigwam, out there in the darkness. After all, our bonfire-to-be was made up of more interesting ingredients than mere planks of wood and bits of straw. There were butter tubs, wooden 'pop' bottle crates, old chairs that customers donated in exchange for a pound of parkin, or a bag of broken biscuits. The chairs were done for in any case, but those Yorkshire villagers had noses for a bargain. We even had a splendid springless settee and a couple of battered armchairs with faded leaf moquette pattern one year, maybe 1935 or '36, earmarked on the outer ring of the pile as first class arena seats for their former owners on the big night.

We simply daren't risk them being stolen, so we refused all invitations out for tea and were on guard weekdays and weekends alike after they came into our possession. Indeed, it would only have needed a couple of broken down nags for our back garden to resemble a gypsy encampment from late October until the final clearing up after 5 November. It's a good job there wasn't much in the way of traffic. The odd horse and cart or two rumbling along with the milk churns could always stand aside until a trailing tree with outstretched branches was fought over in the middle of the road.

The very word 'Yep' struck more terror and chill down our spines than Hitler ever could. Rough serge trousers down to his knees, half length knitted grey socks, substantial boots and dark serge jacket were the perfect camouflage for evenings lighted only intermittently with flickering gas lamps and there were none of those at the back, where the fields were. Occasionally they sought to surprise us, not by stealth, but with warlike, Red Indian yells or Billy Bunterish 'Yarroos' as they hurtled *en masse* over the fence, racing back with whatever came to hand. With Prince snatching at the backs of their trousers, the dog an integral part of our gang.

On the evening itself, dad put trays of large jacket potatoes into our bakehouse oven. When almost ready, willing helpers transferred the 'spuds' to encircle the bonfire. Dad made parkin too, masses of it, as no-one was specifically invited, it was a case of everybody welcome, the more the merrier. Mother enjoyed making treacle toffee which we watched bubbling richly in the big black iron pan. One year she decided the toffee would look pretty in a fluted dish. (We didn't have pyrex then). Without even waiting for the boiling liquid to cool, she poured it straight into the unsuspecting dish and the ensuing crack made her jump back in dismay and amazement, dad asking 'Nay wifey, whativver will t'a do next?', lapsing as usual into broad Yorkshire when events went awry. A debate was carried on

63

Families at New Laithe Hill, Huddersfield, sometime before 1920.

between the two of them whether the toffee was safe to use. Would tiny slivers of glass cut across someone's windpipe as they sucked appreciatively on the jagged succulent hunks? It was eventually declared safe enough and transferred to a more prosaic Yorkshire pudding tin, blackened with age. Then the first casualty of Bonfire Night 1935 was dumped unceremoniously in the dustbin with a disgusted clatter.

Six o'clock was the usual lighting up time for bonfires. Dads would be home from work and ready to put the first match to the pile and to order everybody to 'stand back'. Locals ambled round the back path, muffled up in scarves, overcoats, knitted gloves and caps. VIPs took their places on the springless armchairs and sofa, For all the world like guests at Scarborough Open Air Theatre, waiting to be entertained, wined and dined. They were certainly not wined, but unlimited Tizer, lemonade or dandelion and burdock were available.

Our gang's bonfire party had the edge over Yep's, up there in the Rec, because ours was a free for all as regards refreshments. Lashings of fresh butter to help sink eager mouths into the hot potatoes and the big living kitchen with its roaring fire at the back of the shop for one and all to nip in and 'have a warm' before going out again to join the firework display. There

were always extra boxes of sparklers, rockets, Catherine wheels, silver foun-
tains and other delights in the shop drawers. Any child without, who obviously couldn't afford even a packet of sparklers, was given a box full of
assorted fancily named fireworks. Seeing the wonder and magic in a
shabby youngster's eyes was worth more to dad than money in the till. Nor
had anyone to bother about wiping boots before going into the kitchen.
Linoleum covered the floor and could be easily mopped over next day.
Being house proud didn't make for happiness, having fun and friendship
was always a priority on 5 November or any other time for that matter.

All seven shop cats were safely in the cellar, waiting on beds of potato
sacks until the inferno ended.

Jumping Jacks were feared most of all, those fawn, coiled devils that leapt
here, there and everywhere with terrifying unpredictability. As boys became
older, they found them a good way of 'introducing' themselves to girls.

When the last roast potato was eaten and the splutter and screech of fireworks had become infrequent, satiated neighbours rubbed their tired eyes
and wended their way home. Then we poked the dying embers and went
reluctantly upstairs ourselves to have a last peep from behind the curtains at
the diminishing fires in fields and gardens all around.

Peace would be declared tomorrow between Yep and us and so it continued every November until the 1939-45 war brought a permanent
armistice between our gang and his.

THIRTEEN

Christmas is Coming

Once the Standard firework boxes were out of the way at the shop it was time for us to visit the wholesaler's to buy in for Christmas.

I adored going with mother into town to Beaumonts Warehouse to wander round, after showing our pass proving we had a shop and weren't just the general public. Selecting garishly coloured Chinese lanterns, fancy paper trimmings, balloons and a few 'joy bombs' to put on view at Central Stores. Joy bombs were rather expensive, some as much as 7/6, even in the 1930s and I think mother really had herself in mind when she ordered these, but perhaps the butcher, coalman's wife, or the local doctor might buy one too. Some were shaped like huge snowmen, with tall black hats set at a rakish angle. I remember one of those cotton wool covered joy bombs was a caravan and we kept it for years, filling it with small new delights year after year. We preferred them as a centre piece for the table than any posh floral arrangement. It really was the climax of the meal when they were set off and toys, bracelets, necklaces, and sometimes small Dinkie cars, flew in all directions.

Lots of boxes of crackers and packs of Christmas cards were ordered too and all mother had to do was sign for the goods. Dad received the invoice in the post later, mother and I had the wild spending spree. One Christmas morning I found a huge cardboard box on my bedroom floor and when I opened it there was a life-sized cloth doll, dressed in a flimsy mauve dress with matching poke bonnet. I recalled having seen one exactly like it in Beaumont's warehouse and wondered if Father Christmas patronised them too, all the way from Greenland.

Writing the Christmas cards wasn't a case of shall we or shan't we send any – we racked our brains for more and more people to greet with one. We spread our net wide, it was a pleasure, not a chore, and a whole evening was given over to poring over which to send. The big wooden kitchen table was extended by winding it open with the handle kept in one of the drawers. My brother Philip and I enjoyed the sensation of sitting at opposite ends while a gap appeared in the table between us. Then the two wooden 'leaves' kept behind the cellar door were brought out and fitted into the space. The only other times the table was extended was when we catered for funeral teas or played table tennis on it.

Once the blinds of the shop were drawn, and business was over for the day, the fire was poked into a big blaze and the cards spread out. Our seven cats and Prince, the collie, settled down to snore on the pegged rug and dream of turkey delights to come. Mother consulted the long Christmas card list, written in pencil on a long piece of white 'cap' paper we used for wrapping bread. Each name ticked off after the correct address had been matched with the ones in the address book. 'Compliments of the Season' mother wrote in her large, sprawling handwriting, dipping her pen into the Stevenson's bottle of ink, time after time. Then 'Love, Hilda, Joe, Hazel and Philip' followed by a row of crosses. What satisfaction there was in seeing the piles of stamped envelopes waiting on the big sideboard at bedtime. Next evening after the shop had closed the exciting procedure of extending the table was gone through again. This time for making the decorations. Although some were bought, Philip and I enjoyed gluing those coloured papers together to make chains. Dad stood in the middle of the table with a packet of drawing pins waiting for the paper chains to be handed carefully up. Drawing pins were hammered lightly into place on the ceiling and picture rails, Chinese lanterns opened out, balloons blown up almost to bursting point. How amazing to see what had been contained in a small flat packet reach such mammoth proportions, especially those sausage-shaped ones which, when allowed to quickly expel air, made an aggressive snarling noise which made Prince bark at them and wonder what on earth the world was coming to.

The ball of string kept on the shop counter was brought in to tie firm knots, one of us having to 'just put your finger there' while a knot was tied. We decorated the shop as well, not forgetting strategically placed bunches of mistletoe to which we drew attention when travellers, passing policemen or customers we liked were in the shop.

Some customers paid a small sum each week to ease the burden of buying selection boxes and other gift items outright. One huge deep drawer beneath the 'fittings' in the living kitchen was earmarked solely for Christmas goods 'put by' for customers. Big selection boxes were half a crown in those days. Then there were chocolate cigars, with smart jazzy gold papers round their middles and sweet 'cigarettes' with strawberry pink tips to resemble the lighted end. 'Smokers Outfits' containing these items were very popular – how they would be frowned upon today.

Toy cardboard shops opened out to reveal miniature bottles filled with dolly mixtures and cashews. Tiny celluloid baby dolls with permanently fixed celluloid 'quiffs' over rounded foreheads lay waiting patiently for Christmas Eve. Other favourite stocking fillers were French knitting sets, a wooden reel with four prongs on top, a hook to lift the strands over them, and three or four small balls of brightly coloured mixed shaded wools.

Mother was in her element in the days prior to Christmas. In gleaming white starched overall fresh from the laundry, contrasting with her jet black, marcelled-waved hair, she looked far more desirable to the commercial travellers than any fairy on top of a tree. They breezed in with flurries of snow through the shop door shouting 'Shop! Merry Christmas everybody' then opened their briefcases out on the counter to tantalise mother with a beautifully wrapped presentation pack of Turkish cigarettes (Passing Cloud was a name I recall) or bottles of perfume in exchange for a 'smacker' beneath the mistletoe. That put the seal on business relationships for the following year.

So many ordinary, un-iced 1lb Christmas loaves were turned out in our bakehouse that mother couldn't resist giving one to just about everybody in a surge of festive cheer. So each 'rep' had one pushed into his eager hands and customers who were known to be 'a bit short of the ready' were delighted when mother took yet another one from the seemingly endless flow coming into the shop from the bakehouse on big shallow

---

WHEN IN TOWN — CALL AT

STARKEY'S TRIPE SHOP
IN SHAMBLES LANE
—— WHERE YOU CAN GET THE BEST. ——
Wholesale Works— Firth Street.

CORPORATION OMNIBUS SERVICE
HUDDERSFIELD—SCAPEGOAT HILL

BUS SERVICE.

Hudders-field.	Paddock.	Milns-bridge.	Scape goat Hill.	Golcar.	Milns-bridge.	Paddock.
a.m.	a.m.	a.m.	a.m.	a.m.	a.m.	a.m.
5 50	6 0	6 5	6 35	6 45	6 55	7 0
7 20	7 30	7 35	8 5	8 15	8 25	8 30
8 50	9 0	9 5	9 35	9 45	9 55	10 0
10 20	10 30	10 35	11 5	11 15	11 25	11 30
	p.m.	p.m.	p.m.	p.m.	p.m.	p.m.
11 50	12 0	12 5	12 35	12 45	12 55	1 0
p.m.						
†1 20	1 30	1 35	* 2 5	* 2 15	* 2 25	* 2 30
2 50	3 0	3 5	* 3 35	* 3 45	* 3 55	* 4 0
4 20	4 30	4 35	5 10	5 20	5 30	5 35
5 50	6 0	6 5	* 6 35	* 6 45	* 6 55	* 7 0
7 20	7 30	7 35	* 8 5	* 8 15	* 8 25	* 8 30
8 50	9 0	9 5	* 9 35	* 9 45	* 9 55	*10 0
10 20	10 30	10 35	*11 5	*11 15	*11 25	*11 30

These buses on the return journey into Huddersfield, leave Scapegoat Hill, Golcar, Milnsbridge and Paddock 5 minutes ate than the above times on Saturdays and Sundays.
† First Bus Sundays.

22

A page from the Huddersfield Corporation Tramways & Omnibus Timetable for 1929.

trays. 'I'm sure that tray was full last time I saw it' Dad frequently remarked in a perplexed voice.

Similarly with the bottles of port, supposedly bought for Christmas Day itself. If any elderly, poor, or simply cold looking customer entered the shop in the days leading up to Christmas, mother poured them out 'a little tot to warm the cockles of their hearts.'

The final hour before closing on Christmas Eve was hectic. Extra grocery orders to be collected, mothers and dads slipping in to collect presents for children that had been 'put by.' Smuggling them out in brown paper, hoping that the children would be too tired to begin rooting into 'the groceries.' But even the best kept secrets can go awry. Mrs Cudworth, who had hidden little Audrey's presents at another shop, told us that once Audrey was in bed she had spread them out in the front room ready for filling her daughter's stocking. But Audrey, keyed up with excitement, crept downstairs feeling sick and her mother, realising that everything was on view, without explanation, took off her pinny and flung it over the child's head! Then, guiding her into the kitchen, she administered a spoonful of Fenning's Fever Cure, then shrouded the head again for the return journey upstairs, muttering some excuse about cold draughts on the way up. Audrey told us the story in later years when she became engaged to Philip, my brother.

FOURTEEN

Oh, We Did Like to be Beside the Seaside

'Nay lad, how d'you expect us to carry on if tha shuts shop up, what shall we do for 'us' bread and stuff?' 'You can always go to the Co-op' dad used to reply apologetically after placing the sign 'This shop will be closed Monday and Tuesday, August…' in a prominent position on the counter.

It used to really 'get my mother's goat' as they used to say, only being able to close the shop for a long weekend. 'But if it stays shut any longer customers will get used to going somewhere else' dad reasoned.

So, as a few days were better than no holiday at all, dad wrote off to various private hotels and guest houses, recommended to him by our commercial travellers. When the replies came back they weren't big colour brochures illustrating the merits of the hostelry, but tiny white cards with perhaps 'Piano', 'H & C Water' and '1 Minute from Sea', printed proudly alongside the name of the proprietor, as added inducements. As long as the place had been 'highly recommended' by Hobson's tobacconist's rep, or the Lyon's tea man, or another esteemed gentleman dad knew it would be a place with good grub and decent surroundings.

In the thirties, before the days of going to private hotels we had 'digs', as boarding houses were called, down side streets of seaside resorts and I always felt cheated having to turn aside from the bright lights of the promenade hotels at night time.

We used to pile loads of tins from the shop into a big brown leather case until there was barely room for our clothes. My brother Philip and I sat on top of the suitcase when it was full to try and force the top bit over the lower, while mother repeatedly tried to snap the locks together. Never

Typical small, private hotel, lodging and boarding house cards from the late 1920s.

Sea Front.	Lavatory Basins in Bedrooms.	Piano.

Mrs. CONNOR,

Fitzalan House,

11, Blenheim Terrace,

SCARBOROUGH.

APARTMENTS. Public and Private.

Mrs. Hirst,

15, Barton Avenue,

Off Promenade, South Shore,

Blackpool.

BOARD OPTIONAL.

having aspired to a car, we went in a taxi from Central Stores to the railway station. Even so, I'm sure it was struggling with that heavily laden case that precipitated dad's angina in later years. It seemed to take the rest of the few days for his shoulder to reassume its normal position! Pleasantries with the landlady were exchanged at either Blackpool or Scarborough and we were allocated a couple of shelves in the huge dining room sideboard for foodstuffs. What muttering and accusing eyes there were from other guests should the contents of a marmalade jar thought to be theirs seem unaccountably lower than it should be of a morning! Some of those boarding houses seemed to be as tall as the Eiffel Tower as we wound round and round endless dark stained banisters, dad stopping on each landing with the case to 'get his puff.'

Once inside our 'family bedroom' he threw himself onto the double bed with its brass rails to recover. Philip and I stood on chairs to peer out of the sash window to look for the sea. Only the tops of chimney pots and rows of seagulls gazed back at us. When we complained, mother, reading old newspapers from sometimes as far back as the late twenties which lined the ricketty drawers meant for our clothes, replied 'we haven't come just to stick up here you know.'

My aim was always to buy a new tin bucket and spade and spend as much time as possible on the sands. How galling it was having to wait outside on the bench after meals while parents lingered over cups of tea and cigarettes. 'Telling the tale' with other boarders.

The worst memory of those thirties seaside holidays was trying to find a vacant lavatory midst the labyrinth of landings, all looking the same. Spying from the slightly open bedroom for the magic moment when the door of the WC opened and conveying the good news to an agitated family member hiding behind the door.

Dads enjoyed early morning strolls before breakfast, to buy a newspaper and get a few extra lungs full of ozone before the prom filled up. Shirts open at the neck, grey flannel 'bags' flapping round their legs in the morning breeze – Heaven. Wives usually preferred to make use of the pre-breakfast period applying plenty of Ponds cream, polishing up nails with 'Amami', spitting into the palm of the hand then rubbing some of the pink rouge on. Bright red colour was only for 'common' girls in those days. Devon Violets, Ashes of Roses and Jockey Club were popular scents available from the Nothing Over Sixpence stores. Deciding which cotton or Shantung material dress to wear also took time.

Acquiring a reputation among the other boarders for being 'ever so jolly and easy to get on with' seemed to be a chief preoccupation among them. Weaving their way between the tables each with their bottles of tomato ketchup and HP sauce, nodding a bright greeting to right and left on the way. 'Morning, lovely morning' trying to appear a different person to the one who's agitated face had, only half an hour or so before, kept bobbing in and out behind a bedroom door with monotonous regularity hoping to whizz unobserved along the corridor when a WC door opened, nonchalently

whistling 'A room with a view' or 'Smoke gets in your eyes' or some other hit tune of the period.

Out at last, with the whole of Blackpool or Scarborough stretching enticingly before one, there was the novelty of searching for the most appetising bakery and buying bread and cakes to take back to the lodgings. Also vegetables, and perhaps a joint of meat for the landlady to cook. 'Knock at the kitchen door and give them to Mrs So and So' mother said. How honoured I felt if invited inside that holy of holies, the landladies kitchen!

Joe Taylor striding down the promenade at Blackpool in his swagger coat in the late 1930s.

The Taylors 'getting pally' with others in the digs in Blackpool in about 1930. Joe and Hilda swap partners for the photograph while young Hazel peers at the camera and clutches her comfort blanket.

Then out once again into the brightness of the seaside day, all chores behind us, except the one loved by mother, selecting postcards to send all our customers back home – only a penny stamp and how fast the postal service was. 'We'd better send Mrs Heaton one, or else', mother then sat on a deckchair pencilling the messages while Philip and I piled warm sand into our buckets and dad pored over the newspaper. 'You didn't send us a card!' spat by some forgotten customer felt to mother almost as reprehensible as being accused of murder. A minor holiday disaster once occurred when Philip, impatient to push the cards through the letterbox, raced off and despatched them all without stamps or addresses. 'I can't understand it, I wrote to all of you, one and all'. Mother was most upset, standing on trial behind the shop counter on our return, especially as a major part of the short holiday had been taken up in that one pursuit.

`The holiday pattern never varied; sands in the morning, strolling on the pier or visiting parks or flower gardens in the afternoons. Linking arms with people we knew to sing 'Oh I do like to be beside the seaside' and making a long line of holidaymakers, sometimes a dozen or more wide, taking up the

Joe Taylor (left) and John Hall, the Central Stores shop assistant, on holiday in the 1930s. They are wearing bathing costumes from the drapery drawer at the shop.

whole pavement of the promenade. 'Tiddley-om-pom-pom', we sang, as we jovially bumped into other holidaymakers coming the other way. I suppose that was what was called 'making your own fun' – it *was* fun and free too.

Putting in Peasholme Park at Scarborough was another pleasure. For this I changed from morning shorts and sandals into print dress, white socks and white patent shoes and panama hat for the afternoon.

After staying up late to go to shows (dad always had the job of queuing to book for the Tower Circus or Icedrome) there was always a sing-song round the piano in the boarding house in the front parlour to end the day. There were cream crackers, cheese and a pot of tea if guests were in before a certain time.

Sunday afternoon concerts tended to be a bit highbrow, but so beautiful. Heddle Nash singing 'Come into the garden Maud' I shall never forget, so handsome in dark lounge suit and white starchy looking shirt and bow tie, the contralto and soprano in flowing gowns. Bows and curtseys to the audience. So mannered, yet so humorous as well. Muriel Brunskill and Isobel Baillie were a couple of singers who initiated me into the delights of songs 'Homing' and 'Softly awakes my heart.'

We could have listened forever to the dapper Reginald Dixon playing the organ in the Tower Ballroom, his lively music setting even the oldest feet tapping in rhythm. If it rained that was the time to look for 'A present from Blackpool' or wherever, in the big shops, for those back home. Just before the Second World War some of the commercial trav-

The Arcadian Follies who entertained holidaymakers at Blackpool South Pier in 1936.

Hilda Taylor (right) with Betty Davidson on holiday in Scarborough in the early 1940s.

ellers started spending their holidays 'down south' at posh resorts such as Torquay or Bournemouth, often for as long as a whole fortnight.

As the shop blinds were pulled up on the first day back after our brief holiday, customers were already waiting outside like baying wolves to surge inside Central Stores and resume everyday life. 'Village has felt like a graveyard without yer' was the heartfelt compliment that softened the blow of exchanging sea and sand for the tinkle of the shop doorbell once more. 'Ee, aren't they good!' was the universal pronouncement on seeing the walking pictures of us parading self consciously along the promenade. Or snaps with the Brownie box camera. Oh, that we had taken more!

FIFTEEN

Rabbits & Records

Sam, one of the village lads in our locality during the Second World War, made quite a bit of spending money breeding rabbits and selling them. With food shortages, most people fattened them up for the table. To me, that was absolutely unthinkable. Bunny, a large, wild-looking Flemish Giant and a timid little black and white doe we called Beauty, immediately elipsed all thoughts of Hitler, Churchill, doodle-bugs or anything else. They were mine to be worshipped and molly-coddled, forever, I hoped. Sam and Jim, his brother, built a hutch for them which we placed on raised bricks at the back of our bakehouse. It would be warm for them there. And they had a comforting view of the green fields and woods beyond, in the hours I was away at school.

How odd I would have been thought by today's fifteen year olds! Spending all my free time after homework with a couple of rabbits. Though they entailed a lot of work, I felt fulfilled and happy in my service of them. Pretending that they were a wealthy married couple and I was the lady who earned half a crown an hour by cleaning for them. It was gratifying also to watch the eagerness on their small pointed faces when offered fresh green dandelion leaves in springtime and the way they leapt about over the farmer's field at the back of our garden while I cleaned out the hutch. Monday evenings were the highlight of our week. My parents used the free theatre pass given them for showing the bill of the week on the counter in our shop. On cold winter evenings I carried the hutch into the rambling kitchen. The seven cats having first been shooed down into the cellar. After a preliminary sniffing and wrinkling of noses, Bunny and Beauty cautiously stepped out into the home-made pegged rug. There they

Hazel, at twelve years old, in the garden at Central Store, 1939.

stretched their legs out full length, savouring the warmth from the blazing coal fire set in the shining black leaded Yorkshire range. Who says animals are only used to living outside and can't appreciate the warmth?

The rabbits loved to dance. If there was no suitable programme of music on the wireless I had a large stock of records to play on my old gramophone. All three of us adored those private performances, Bunny, the buck, appreciated music especially. Leaping nigh half way to the ceiling, like some woolly male ballerina and performing a mid-air twist before coming to rest on the rug. Eyes bulging at his own prowess, until another chord struck his fancy. Beauty, my pretty little black and white doe, was more docile. Preferring simply to relax serenely for most of the evening in front of the fire. Dreaming dreams of love, I'm sure. I often thought she'd have enjoyed a little bit of knitting, to pass away her caged hours.

I thought Beauty loved Heddle Nash singing 'Your tiny hand is frozen,' from The fair maid of Perth. I'm sure they adored Anne Zeigler and Webster Booth duets and the soaring voice of Richard Tauber. Halfway through the evening, we all had our suppers together. Me sitting on the rug with a mug of cocoa and biscuits, Bunny and Beauty wrinkling their noses into saucers of bran and oats and drinks of water.

I insisted they be brought into the kitchen on chilly afternoons too, if it was too cold for them to have a gambol in the garden. Visiting aunts and uncles frequently looked askance at rabbits on the rug. But I was determined that Bunny and Beauty had equally as much right to their weekend comforts as had the humans. So there they stayed, while I kept a weather eye open for marauding cats, and a brush and shovel close at hand for any small black 'accidents' on the rug or oilcloth.

After a few months of this, to my mind idyllic way of life, tragedy struck. One Monday teatime after school I dashed round to the hutch as usual. Horror rooted me momentarily to the spot. It couldn't be true, was I imagining it? I looked again and closer. The wire netting at the front of the hutch hung down, limp and torn. Bunny and Beauty lay together, their pretty little heads a couple of inches away from their bodies. Dad, wiping a tear from his eye with his white apron, supposed that a stoat or weasel must have gnawed its way into the hutch and attacked their throats. We buried them in the henyard, under the old apple tree where other much-loved childhood companions lay. Sam and the other village children assembled for the funeral service, conducted by Philip my brother. Choking back the tears, we erected a small wooden cross, with the names etched on it with a penknife.

Had I been misguided? Would they have suffered less if they had been treated as other, more ordinary, rabbits then killed by human hand for the table? That night my pillow was soaked with tears. How would I struggle through the long, long years ahead? Live through my twenties, thirties, even forties, without my dear pets? It seemed unthinkable. Yet, as after every death, every parting, life goes on. Other loves, other tragedies, come along to bowl us over with the same intensity of feeling. Or maybe not quite so bad as our first introduction to death, the death of a pet. In our adolescence we feel that we, and our family and belongings, are quite, quite indestructable and immune from the ravages of life. Throughout the years I have found that after a bereavement, writing about it, telling my diary, writing poems to the dear departed (as I did to my rabbits, and still have them) helps to cleanse out the bitterness, the hurt. And I am left with only vivid, happy memories of the characters, both animal and human, that have briefly touched my own life. Plus positive proof that the human spirit does surmount grief and that time does heal. In my 1942 diary I wrote, in pencil:

May 1st. Bad luck day. Prince got a bit better. My two little rabbits, Bunny and Beauty, killed by rats (or something) with their heads off. I am still crying. So is Prince.

Bunsen & Beauty
In memory of my two pals!
Bunny was so bold and gay
Until the morning, 1st of May
When he and his little sweetheart, so had to part
But not from each other, just breaking my heart
Hand in hand, paw in paw, to glory they went after a life short but
    happily spent.
My pets, my darlings,
Beauty and Buns,
Goodbye, adieu,
Till we meet in heaven above.

May 1st 1942
Hazel Taylor

SIXTEEN

Beginning a Diary

My daily diary keeping habit began in 1942, when I was given a small pocket diary. I was fourteen, a pupil at Greenhead High School for Girls. 'PRIVATE' is written in pencil, in the inside cover. Indeed, the whole year is written in pencil. Personal memo included National Registration Number KFGV 1874, size in boots, 5, in gloves, 6, Hats? Collars ? Cash summary-balance from last year £1 1s 0d.

Letter rate then was $2\frac{1}{2}$d not exceeding 2oz, exceeding 2oz but not 4oz, 3d. For every additional 2oz or fraction thereof, $\frac{1}{2}$d. Postcards could be sent for 2d, reply postcards 4d.

The distressing deaths of my rabbits, the first deaths ever recorded in a diary of mine was on 1 May. The 8 May is pencilled round, it was Jack Fox's birthday. He was the dancing master and owner of Fox's Academy, where school form friends Edith, Joan Dunworth, and a few others, occasionally went to learn the waltz, quick step, foxtrot and Paul Jones. Oh, the crush we all had on Jack! He wore black evening suit, starched whiter than white shirt, black bow tie, Cherry Blossomed black dancing shoes, gleaming with a magnificent polish only Cherry Blossom could impart. His hair, parted down the middle, was Brylcreemed to an equally high lustre. When not dancing he watched his pupils from a vantage point by the radiogram, always with a cigarette dangling from his immaculately clean fingertips. He had dimples when he smiled. Oh, the magic of first love…

We danced to Victor Sylvestor records and when Jack sauntered across the gleaming floor, first stubbing out his cigarette in an ashtray, my heart pounded. 'Come along, my little flower' he addressed the chosen pupil. What a wonderful way of addressing a young lady when her name escapes the memory! Oh, the sheer heaven to be pressed closely against that snowy white chest as he manoeuvred our feet, in silver or gold dancing shoes, around the floor. So different to the rough texture of khaki battle dress, when soldiers on leave asked, 'May I have this dance?'

I think Jack had a bad heart, he was exempt from active service. Sometimes, unable to bear the intervening days before we saw him again, one of us took a deep breath, dialled the Dancing Academy number and enquired when classes were (anonymously) just for the intoxication of hearing his voice. Jack lived near Greenhead High School and if occasionally we saw him walking down the road, as we went up to school in our uniform of navy and blue striped blazer, panama hat with blue and navy band, satchel, hockey sticks or tennis rackets in tow, I felt myself blushing madly and heart bumping like a caged tiger.

First entry in my 1942 diary reminds me that I played hockey with Philip, my brother and Prince our dog in the field behind our house. In the evening going to the Regent to see Charles Boyer in the film 'Back Street.' We walking home in the blackout, with dimmed torches.

School holidays were looked forward to in winter especially because it meant I could stay in bed reading in the morning, not getting up until mother called 'dinner's ready.' A book I was reading then was called *Gay Nights*. Not the meaning gay has today, but not recommended for Greenhead High School for Girls reading either.

Mother spent many evenings darning socks which were stretched over the wooden 'mushroom' to enable criss-crossing the worn part with wool. 'Make do and mend' was part of our war effort – unlike the throwaway society of today.

4th January 1942. 'Philip and his pal Roger Smith [who went in the RAF] played 'Dogs' in the afternoon for money!

Good heavens, next day, again 'Got up late'. Then played cards with Philip and Bernard, a soldier who used to visit us. Read 'For Men Only' magazine in the privacy of our front room above the shop after tea. There was a thin layer of snow.' Square-toed bootees were fashionable. Next day mother and I bought a pair each, covered in black fur. They were wildly expensive – I think they were about seven guineas. When we emerged, having decided to wear them there and then, we could hardly stop giggling every time we looked down and saw four square toed bootees marching in unison. We had tea in the Ritz cinema.

Philip, a clerk at the National Provincial Bank, was on fire watching duty there on Sunday night. Mother warned him to 'look after himself' with the underlying meaning, never mind the fire, save your own life.

How we shuddered in terror in the 'one and nines', when we went to see Boris Karloff in *Juggernaut*. Only returning to reality and safety after calling at the fish and chip shop and enjoying eating from the paper bag as we walked home in the frosty night air.

My diary noted that a pipe burst in the house on the twentieth. Fortunately, the plumber, one of our customers, only lived a few doors away. He came at once to repair it, and was rewarded with a ('keep it quiet') bit of butter, besides how much it cost, for his prompt attention.

After homework 'speedily attended to' on the evening of the twenty-second, walked in the snow up the hill to the Rialto cinema with mother and Mildred, our shop assistant. One of the films was *Victory*.

There wasn't room to write much in the inch space allowed for each daily entry. 'School' usually began it, followed by a note about the weather. 'Snow almost gone and warm to say it is January' on the twenty-third. Although it was mother's forty-first birthday there was nothing special by way of celebration. I knitted a khaki balaclava, Philip read, mother and Mildred mended a few stockings while listening to the wireless. Dad was at the local club playing billiards.

There were plenty of potatoes in the war years, so home made chips were a regular and never failing supper time delight. Dad's cousin Annie came to tea and to collect her rations on a Saturday every fortnight. It was policy to 'ration' with a couple of different grocers for different items, so as to be considered if there was an extra delivery of anything.

It was cold in the unheated bedrooms, apart from a little gas fire, sitting up reading in bed, but a pair of fingerless mittens and an old coat round my shoulders served well enough as I read Quentin Durwood on Sunday morning.

We took Prince for 'a long walk through the wood' when it turned out 'cold but sunny'. We had a 'charlady', as domestic helps were then called, who 'helped put down a new oilcloth in the bathroom' next day. We played on the frozen reservoir in the field behind the shop, pretending to be skater Sonja Heni.

The routine of school was tempered once a week, on Tuesdays, by meeting mother at four fifteen at Rushworth's corner in town, bulging satchel over my shoulder, for tea in a cafe. Afterwards we went perhaps to the Kingsway, Collinson's, or the Princess. On 14 January my diary records that we saw *49th Battalion* in the Princess cinema.

How exciting it was when village 'boys' who had been called up into the services popped in to see us when they were on leave. John, the shop assistant before Mildred, appeared in his khaki battle dress one Saturday with the usual 'could you spare a packet of cigs?'

'No snow has stuck all week' my entry says for Monday 26 January 1942. 'School. Played in field with Prince till dusk. Homework. Knitted while listening to the wireless.'

On Tuesday 27 January, after school at four, I raced down town to see mother, anxiously patrolling up and down outside Rushworth's corner. Tea in Whiteley's café was followed by the Princess cinema to see Anna Neagle in *Sunny*. I enjoyed it very much indeed. Next day, after school and homework, I made a gardening plan from a book. Visions of feeding the family with a constant flow of fresh vegetables and 'Digging For Victory' was the spur. Philip went to the YMCA down Deighton Road, Mother and Dad to the Palace Variety show in town using the free pass for displaying the programme in the shop.

Thursday 29 January, school, homework, 'mending' with mother. Philip to the ATC (Air Training Corps), dad playing billiards at the club.

Friday 30 January, school. Snow, one inch. Mother to Mrs Carson's on Browning Road after tea.

Saturday 31 January, read Quentin Durwood in bed. Played in field with Prince. Supper at Grandma's down Whitacre Street. Don't know how she bears it living all alone in that dark old stone house, with that big, baleful stag's head on opening the front door.

SEVENTEEN

Grandad's Henyard

Grandad had a piece of gritty land to the left of the house and shop which he had had fenced off to make a henyard. A couple of huts were erected, perches nailed to the walls, and nesting boxes placed round the sides. We had a dozen Rhode Island hens and a russet brown cock with shiny feathers and floppy red comb. This cock had an arrogant demeanour and strutted about as though he patrolled a jewelled harem instead of a bit of gritty Yorkshire soil. I loved to feed them before going to school in a morning. We had a tall round container that must have been as old as the hills for the smooth, golden Indian corn . As I approached the hens I called 'Chuck, chuck, chuck, chuck!' and the inhabitants of the yard flew to meet me while grandad called 'make sure you latch the henyard door behind you now.'

Being enclosed with that lot had something of the atmosphere of being in a lion's den. All pecking and flying up against one's legs. With such challenging thoughts I rolled the corn between my fingers before scattering it high in the air. 'Chuck, chuck, chuck, chuck' and the eager feathery diners clustered round my ankle socks pushing each other out of the way. Then I went back into the kitchen to wash out the white enamel, blue rimmed drinking bowls and refill them with water. I thought it must have been monotonous for them, never tasting tea, or coffee, or wine.

Then came the fruits of my labours, the game of hide-and-seek for eggs. The anticipation of feeling around in the dry straw in the huts for the lovely warm, oval eggs, some brown, others white. Some with bits of hen dirt and downy feathers sticking to the shells but each to me a miracle and, I suppose, to the clucking hens as well who gathered round to see what I was up to. I carried the eggs into the house as proudly as though I'd laid them myself.

Grandad and Grandma Taylor in the garden at Central Stores.

Saturday mornings were my idea of heaven. Especially so on warm, blue and gold mornings in Spring, when I spring cleaned the hen huts. They were my dolls' houses, the hens my living dolls. Armed with old bucket, brush and shovel and Prince the dog as overlooker to see the job was done right, I was supremely happy. I piled the old, soiled straw in a heap in my own patch of garden, in the walled ground at the side of the shop, ready to be burned. Propped the hut doors wide open with bricks or stones to let gusts of clean fresh air in, piled sweet smelling new hay and straw in the boxes before putting them back. Sometimes I drawing-pinned old net curtains up at the windows, and pinned a couple of drawings on the walls. Care had to be taken before darkness fell to drop down the horseshoe shaped entrance to each hut, in case of marauding foxes from the fields and woods beyond.

Up at the top end of my own garden was a disused closet or privy as the old folk used to call the outside WCs. The wooden seat, square and wide, was just right for a spot of relaxation on after school, to sit and watch my garden grow. All those straight lines of peas, carrots and lettuces. Just right for shelter, that old red brick building, in case of a sudden storm. No longer in use for its original purpose, it was ideal for my den, indeed, in my own mind I considered it a grandiose summer house, where I could sit and contemplate life in general. I had visions of growing vegetables in such abundance that we'd be able to sell them in the shop without recourse to buying them from wholesale greengrocers. We'd be rich due to my efforts in no time at all.

I'd make up to Dad, with my 'smallholding' for the money wasted by mother in allowing customers or anyone at all to serve themselves in the shop and put their own money in the till, to save her bothering, not to mention the pounds that were wasted every week in paying for work that she could have done herself. It was a good dream. One that I could work at physically and, in time, I thought, make it a reality. Of course, I wasn't then ten, and hadn't even gone in for my eleven-plus exams, but dreams can come true. Even those hatched on an old privy seat. Besides the allotment and smallholding, another idea took form on my ninth birthday. When John, our shop assistant, put his woodworking prowess to work and made a proper swing for me in the henyard. I asked for it to be erected there, it had thick, proper wooden posts which were dug deep into the ground, so that I'd be a bit of company for the hens.

Our swings before that had been primitive, a cushion flopped over a rope and suspended from a branch of the apple tree which grew at the far end of the henyard, by the field. One's anatomy, even at eight or nine, couldn't put up with such discomfort for very long at a time. But now there was a stout wooden framework, with a couple of sturdy iron hooks on the cross bar and a proper shop-bought wooden seat, with strong, plaited white ropes to hold.

Frequently, the swing and cross bar were adorned with a hen or two having a siesta, or proclaiming their presence to the world at large, or treating themselves to a better view of the surrounding countryside. There were always white and black hen droppings on the seat, but I didn't mind. I could knock them off. As long as they were enjoying themselves, that was all that mattered.

So, with the advent of my real swing proclaimed abroad, our henyard became the most popular playing out spot in the whole village. While the adjoining field bristled with the pathetic faces of local children who could never hope for a swing of their own. Sometimes, they might 'nick' an old tyre and use that in the woods, suspended from a bit of old rope, but that wasn't the same as a real, shop-bought swing, was it? There they stood, after school, munching huge chunks of bread and jam for their teas and begging 'can ah 'ave a go on yer swing, eh?'

Only one child could be satisfied at a time, so arguments cropped up constantly about who'd had the longest 'go.' More often than not the henyard ended up as a boxing ring, with another go on the swing as a reward for the winner. I sometimes wondered if it belonged to me at all.

However, the get rich idea was to make our henyard a proper play-ground, just like the one in the 'rec', the recreation ground at the back of the Woolpack pub where most of us found out all we knew about the difference between girls and boys. Where Ida regularly pulled her knickers down to let the boys 'have a squint' for a Riley's toffee roll. She was mad about Riley's toffee rolls.

Of course, we didn't have to pay to go on the amusements in the 'rec' but I proposed to levy a charge when my playground was made. Each day after school I set to work on my plan. For a see-saw I balanced an old plank across a few stones, piled on top of one another. Discarded wooden butter tubs made credible boats, or so I thought. The trouble was that the hens leapt in before any of us had a chance to and there wasn't a lake. I tried digging a big wide pit and filling it up with water but it always seeped away into the soil at the sides. It was back breaking work too.

The girls complained about getting splinters in their knickers when on the see-saw but they were always back next day for another go on it.

Bribery and corruption was rampant. I had offers of help with cleaning the hen huts out in exchange for ten minutes on the swing. Offers of sticky toffees which as often as not had been stuck to the insides of lads' trouser pocklets for goodness knows how long. There were even magnificent, self-denying offers of apple cores.

But offsetting the genuine offers of payment were the muttered threats. 'Ah'll bash yer 'ead in Taylor if yer don't let me have a go.' 'Give us a go on t' swing, else ah'll git yer behind t' lavs at school tomorrer.'

Thus the once white ropes became jammy and grimy and often I longed for the dark winter evenings, when the ropes and seat were brought in, except for occasional fine weekends. So that get rich quick dream failed. I felt too sorry for my friends, yes, and my

Hazel by the rhubarb patch, and eating a piece of rhubarb, in the garden at Central Stores in 1938.

88

Hazel with a small friend on the henyard swing in 1936.

enemies, who could never achieve private swing status. So I usually let them all in. With the strict warning 'don't forget to close the door behind you, or the hens will escape. We don't want them run over in the road.' On the odd occasions when I had the swing to myself, those rare, sweet moments before breakfast, or a snatched few minutes after dinner before dashing back to school, I still dreamt of charging an entrance fee. Perhaps I was the twin soul of Billy Butlin.

If the idea worked I need never bother about pursuing a career on leaving school. Or passing examinations. I'd be able to make enough money from my henyard-cum-amusement park to allow me to live in luxury until I married. Alas, just when I'd definitely decided on that scheme, and mentally lined up John to knock up a wooden rocking horse for the playground, a face would peer enviously over the fence. Something inside my stomach did a somersault. How could I charge so much as a button or a pin to someone so obviously deprived of all the material comforts of this world as Dorothy? All she had in abundance was nits. Or Sam, whose dad was a sailor and his mother became fat and produced yet another brother or sister every time he went back to sea, the kids we gave our outgrown clothes to.

Besides, Sam was OK, he was the village dare-devil. He once dared to pick up one of Ben Clay's great, hard slabs of sun-baked horse manure and eat it for a dare. He had to earn his spending money by stunts like that, poor beggar. But I suppose he thought it worth it for the rousing cheers that went up from the other lads as his cheeky face split into a grin after his dare was over. I rushed into the shop and gave him a small bottle if Tizer to take the taste away, but he said that he liked it.

Anyway, I decided, what good are riches? I had my swing, a head full of daydreams, and all our shop's riches to go at and there's no joy on earth comparable to a sunny Spring day, a comic to read, and the gentle to-and fro-ing of a swing. Or the energetic sense of adventure after working oneself up to the sky and nearly turning turtle over the cross bar. So I decided I would marry a rich man when I grew up, it would save a lot of bother.

EIGHTEEN

Cheery Charwomen

During the war we employed a succession of charwomen to help out at the shop. John had gone into the army and so had Jimmy the baker. Anyone at all, whatever their age, was an asset if they could 'keep the wheels turning.' First, there was bustling Mrs Bentley with her sharp, determined looking elbows and a vast expanse of body both back and front – she had a way of steamrollering over all obstacles. Even Hitler would have had to shift had he encountered her bulk. Everything, inaminate or animate wilted beneath her onslaught. Cats learned to be fleet of paw to escape the black lace-up brogues belonging to Mrs Bentley, as she thundered about in her sacking apron with string round the middle – a waist it could not be termed. One could liken her, without being unkind (because they are capable and thorough in their work) to a carthorse. Mrs Bentley even had a forelock hanging over her faintly furrowed forehead. The rest of her shortish, mousy brown hair was firmly held behind her ears with a couple of big strong 'Kirby' grips. She preferred to work without her false teeth. Her jaws clamped together in an even more flat out, determined manner without them. Her mouth looked like a straight washing line, with no cupid's bow or unnecessary shapes like that. Mrs Bentley could turn her strong, reddened hands to anything. From scrubbing the wooden boards of a shop floor, cleaning outside drains until they shone like new, to 'lending a hand' with icing trays full of Queen buns. Her strength and capacity for hard work was incredible. Donkey work as she called it, was her hobby as well as her livelihood. Good plain cooking came within her compass also. Lots of potatoes could be peeled in no time, and sloshed into the big black pan. Apple pies and gooseberry, as long as they were on a large scale, were child's play to her. Whether making them for her own family or for us. Every job was attacked with gusto. Her pleasure was work and more work, it was her God. Scouring doorsteps, washing windows with big, swishing strokes of her wash leather were fine but sitting with her feet up would have been anathema to our Mrs Bentley.

So viciously did she ram into her chores that the effort forced her serviceable black woollen stockings to wrinkle round her wide legs. When she bent over a drain, showing her pale pink flannelette knee-length bloomers, one could imagine that a Bamforth comic postcard had sprung to buxom life.

One essential quality all our charwomen had in common was that they were local and always available. They shopped at our shop, had hardly any interests outside home and family, so to be called upon in an emergency down at the shop made them feel much more important in the world. They were an essential part of the war effort. Besides, half a crown an hour was half a crown, and could buy quite a lot. Mrs Bentley had been known to 'take over' in the shop if mother or dad had an urgent appointment in town. Or she'd come in for a couple of hours to weigh up flour, or, in dire emergency, she once came to act as midwife to Pussy Bakehouse until the vet arrived.

Poor Pussy had laboured on the rug for ages, but the enormous body inside her refused to emerge. Mrs Bentley tugged, as gently as she

could, her elbows splayed out and her own body crouched encouragingly over Pussy Bakehouse. This was one occasion when brute force was not enough. 'It's nooan gonna come,' she kept panting, 'ah've nivver come across owt as 'okkard' as this afoor'. Eventually, when Miss Milner the lady vet arrived, who was once Head Girl at Greenhead High School, Mrs Bentley was detailed to hold Pussy's top half

The sort of underwear favoured by some Huddersfield ladies in the not too distant past! An assistant at Mary Riley-Dibb's shop in Huddersfield market holds up a pair for inspection.

while she deftly and speedily removed the dead, headless obstruction that looked more like a rat than a kitten.

Events such as these coloured our charwomen's lives. They adored being summoned to Central Stores, where 'summat allus seemed to be going off.' However, even battleships succumb to the ravages of time. We were astounded one day to learn that big, strong Mrs Bentley had died suddenly. Of course, she wouldn't have had the patience to lie in bed and die slowly.

Then we employed poor, deferential Mrs Crow, more to do her a favour perhaps than ourselves. She was aptly named, as her nose, in her thin pale face was beaked, her garments inevitably of deepest black. She had an invalid husband and any little perks she was given, apart from the normal hourly payment of half a crown, added a little lustre to her pale and weary eyes. A bag of broken biscuits, a madeira loaf with a corner knocked off, a bulged tin of soup or beans, all helped to ease the daily grind of her existence. It's strange how often the most unattractive exterior hides the kindest spirit. When Mrs Crow applied for the job of charwoman at the shop, she hardly looked a likely candidate. Five foot nothing in height and her legs were grotesque. Though she contrived to wear long skirts to keep her legs covered, they still failed to disguise completely her abnormality. From the knees downwards, both legs pointed in the same direction. Mrs Crow lifted her skirts one day and showed us what either rickets or malnutrition had effected in her childhood. When she walked, it was like watching a small ship being blown with the wind, off course, but she arrived where she wanted to be in the end. Nevertheless, legs askew, shabby headscarf forever hiding her sparsely covered head, Mrs Crow was helpful and kindly to everyone. She called us all 'lovey' even Dad, her employer.

The cats were all 'sweet little things' even if one was taken short beneath the kitchen sideboard. The sweet little thing couldn't help it, and Mrs Crow sailed to the sink for a bucket full of hot water and a cloth and proceeded to mop it up.

Ill health finally caught up with Mrs Crow, sadly, and with tears in her eyes, she apologised profusely about 'not feeling up to' carrying on with the extra work. Besides, her husband was needing more attention at home. Her only pleasure, besides her work, would have to be curtailed. She did, however, know of a young woman who'd be glad to earn a bit extra. Lots of the young and energetic women were at that time in the forces, munitions or land army.

Una, as the 'new' charwoman-to-be was named, had a couple of babies, but would be glad of an opportunity to help out with the family finances. Her husband was in the navy, but her mother would be looking after the youngsters while Una went out doing a bit of charring.

Una was round and plump, but in a much softer way than our bustling Mrs Bentley. Placid and easy going, the pace of her dusting matched her unruffled temperament. It's a good job some of these ladies we employed weren't paid on piece work! She was something of an amateur fortune teller too, which activity consumed quite an amount of her time with us. Whenever there was a break for tea or coffee, and there were plenty, everyone was invited to have their cups read. We all looked on it as a bit of a joke, but even those who didn't believe it wouldn't have missed the touch of magic that Una's reading gave to the day. When her family grew up and married, she became a spiritual healer. Now she has lots of successes to show for her untiring willingness to help and she doesn't ever charge a penny for her time and talents. She still looks as happy, calm and radiant as when she used to enhance our lives at the shop. Never once did we see her frown or shout in anger.

Always Una presented the smiling face and dancing eyes. She hadn't much then in the way of material things, but how much more she had than most in her joyous acceptance of life! A shining personality is worth a hundred shines on the furniture.

So, 'charwomen' as once we called these treasures, came in all shapes and sizes and life at Central Stores would have been the poorer without them.

NINETEEN

On the Sunny Side of the Street

~≈~

We didn't have to endure transistors and taped 'music' while shopping in the thirties. But that didn't mean to say we were entirely without song and dance as we brought home the bacon. John, our shop assistant before the Second World War took him off to the Middle East, was a Bing Crosby fan and crooned all day long behind the counter. 'Shuffle off to Buffalo' 'White Christmas' (even in the midst of a heatwave) and 'Deep in the Heart of Texas' serenaded customers as they pondered twixt Fox's ginger biscuits or Huntley and Palmers mixed creams. The biscuits were loose, in big tins. Customers used to 'try one' to see which they liked best. John stood, paper bag in hand, quite happy to wait until the decision was made, in a dream world of his own. Customers who may be wondering how they could manage till next pay day quickly caught the mood, smiles lit up their faces, hope swelled into their hearts, as they twirled round the shop floor partnered by mother and John. 'I used to walk in the shade, with those blues on parade, But I'm not afraid, This Rover crossed over, if I never have a cent I'll be rich as Rockefeller, Gold dust at my feet, On the sunny side of the street.'

The impromptu dance over, a few groceries put 'on tick' till pay day and a bag of broken biscuits pushed into their basket 'for a bit of fun', few left the shop feeling as miserable as when they'd come in.

Dad never mastered the quickstep and foxtrot. He wasn't really interested, though he was as mad about singing as the rest of them. Therefore, when everyone was doing it, dancing, during the 1930s mother went for private lessons a couple of afternoons a week and roped the willing shop assistant in for evening dance sessions in the front room above the shop.

After crooning Ba-ba-ba-boo throughout the day and twitching from left to right across the shop floorboards attending to customers, John was still keen to dance to the records after the shop had closed. He had an enviable knack of being able to balance on his heels, from side to side. I thought it marvellous! He even found time to try and instruct me in the correct verbal hesitations of 'Goodnight Vi-e-e-e-na, you city of a million memories.' I never could get it to his satisfaction but it gave him the perfect excuse to keep warbling it himself. Other times the air would be alive with whistling but people seem to have lost that art these days.

This was the time when the world was agog about the romance of Mrs Simpson and the King. Mother read all about it in the papers, and took photographs of Mrs Simpson, and sometimes film star Kay Frances, to the hairdresser to see if they could copy them on her. She had an obsession for having her photograph taken too, draped, or wearing her white fox fur, at a studio in town called Greaves.

John was also adept at woodwork and in his spare time made a gramophone cabinet in which we housed our records. We proudly stood it alongside the new radiogram up in the front room. Frequently, mother couldn't contain herself until the shop had closed to begin dancing. She used to run upstairs and play a few dance records, inspiring whoever was down below in the shop to grab whoever was available.

'You oughta take it up Joe lad,' dad was urged, as Florrie the coalman's wife or Mrs Wood the fish and chip shop man's wife whirled him round the creaking floorboards, 'They say t'fat 'uns make t'best gliders.' Best of all, I enjoyed the evening dance sessions, when I was safely tucked up in bed, next door to the 'Palais de Danse.' Always, the session began with the sparkling Lullaby of Broadway. Probably mistakenly assuming that that would send Philip and me to sleep. Then followed spirited renderings of 'I gotta a rainbow around my shoulders, and a sky of blue above' with accompanying heavy-footed thuds round the room. The rainbow fitting like a glove led onto smoochy melodies such as 'Ramona, I'll meet you by the waterfall,' and 'Tina, when the leaves are falling, won't you come back to me.' The one record which invariably had me crying into my pillow was, 'Old faithful, we've roamed the range together, Old faithful, in every kind of weather, when your roundup days are over, there'll be pastures white with clover, for you, Old faithful pal of mine.' As John and mother pranced round and round crooning 'Giddy Giddy Up,' I thought of poor old carthorse Ben, outside in the cold field and wished he could be brought inside, to warm himself in front of the fire. Halfway through the evening, when the dancers needed 'a breather' a smoke, and a bit of refreshment, they listened to monologues and drank dandelion and burdock or Tizer. One of our prized records was Stanley Holloway reciting the 'Lion and Albert', another was 'Sam, Sam, Pick up thi Musket' and another one was about Henry the Eighth and his wives. One of which 'walked the draughty corridor, for miles and miles around, with her head, tucked, underneath her arm, at the midnight hour.'

I breathed a sigh of relief when that was over and they began thudding round again, interrupted spasmodically by sudden yells of anguish if John's heavy boots came down on mother's silver dancing shoes. Then off back into the room next door to put on another dance tune. There was no need for alcohol, the music itself was intoxicating enough.

Philip and I occasionally called out for a request song. What bliss to lie there, all safe and sound, waiting for the first crackly sounds of a favourite record going round the grooves. We knew that the evening was drawing to a close when John put on, and accompanied with his own singing,

> *Oh give me a home,*
> *Where the buffalo roam,*
> *And the deer and the antelope play*
> *Where seldom is heard, a discouraging word*
> *And the skies are not cloudy all day.*

So authentically did our shop assistant croon and emulate a famous cowboy of the time that when the front room door opened for him to leave I fully expected to hear a white horse snorting its way downstairs with him. Dad never bothered to learn dancing himself, he was happy enough playing billiards after the shop was closed, down at the club. He knew Hilda never need be short of a dancing partner. Besides, he maintained, with an indulgent grin, that she led him a big enough dance as it was.

TWENTY

Speech Day & the Pork Pie Man

~≋~

While I was just at the onset of having crushes on the opposite sex, mother was being paid court to by the pork pie man. He travelled for the best pork pie makers in town and considered himself very genteel, he enjoyed the theatre and classical music and wore a little green/red feather in the brim of his tweed trilby. Dad couldn't stand him. 'I can't see what you see in that bugger,' he constantly repeated when mother, all flushed and bright eyed, stood at the shop door blowing kisses to the pork pie man as he returned to his car. He hadn't been called up because there was something physically wrong with him. 'I'll bet there's nowt wrong with his you know what,' dad ranted, after mother accepted an invitation to a cultural weekend in Harrogate with him and his daughter. 'Don't worry Mr Taylor, we'll look after Mrs Taylor, the change will do her good' the pork pie man reassured dad. He wore very thick glasses and had to peer through them to see anything at all, so dad probably thought he was imagining things that mother fancied him. More likely she enjoyed his flattery, as she always did when men said complimentary things to her.

Dad was now suffering from angina and the stress of the forthcoming cultural weekend, with him left behind to look after Philip and me, was obviously not helping matters. He was getting to the stage where he'd said he would 'swing for the bugger' and nights were peppered with arguments from Mother and Dad's bedroom. No indeed, it was becoming increasingly clear to me that all the beauty in songs and music didn't belong in real life at all.

In December our school held its Speech Day and for weeks beforehand the junior choir, of which I was a member, and senior choir had

Hazel (left) on her sixteenth birthday in 1943 with friend Hazel Crowther. She wears an RAF badge on her lapel. Both attended Greenhead High School for Girls.

stayed behind after school to rehearse carols and other contributions. Speech Day coincided with the day mother went to Harrogate with the pork pie man and his daughter and I felt most disappointed that she wouldn't be there to hear the result of all those weeks of work. The Girls' Grammar School that I attended during those war years lived up to the musical traditions of the town in having an excellent junior and senior choir. How could it be otherwise, when Miss Spikes, the music mistress, fired up everyone with her own enthusiasm? Middle aged, ruddy cheeked, with bright piercing blue eyes, 'Spikey' had no need to bother about dress to impress all who encountered her. In autumn and winter terms, spring too if the weather remained chilly, she wore a loose tailored green tweed suit with crocheted green blouse and flat brown brogues. In summer she wore a simple shirtwaister green cotton dress. Iron grey hair never wavered from a centre parting, drawn back from the strong face into a bun at the nape of her neck. She always carried, along with her music case, a capacious brown leather handbag which was, like herself, for service rather than frivolity. Gentleman, I felt sure, held no interest for her whatsoever, unless, of course, they shared her passion for music. She lived for music, and her dedication never proved itself more than on the annual Speech Day, which always took place in the Town Hall, where the renowned Huddersfield Choral Society hold many of their concerts.

There was a special music room at the High School, right at the top of the building. A small, enchanted room, full of books about music, busts of composers, looking sternly out from their stone faces onto the generations of girls who came and went. The dominating presence, however, was Miss Spikes the music mistress.

The room was reached by a twisting staircase which always made me think of going up into an enchanted tower. Containing a different atmosphere completely to the hectic workaday world of Central Stores. Indeed, I would have disowned living there at the time if I could. The aspirations of the school, and especially that ethereal music, seemed light years away from the ordinary folk who patronised our shop. Then again, some of my form friends' fathers were doctors, or mill owners, and although I knew my dad was equally, if not more brainy than their dads, somehow being the daughter of a village grocer didn't have the cachet or standing with our headmistress as coming from a more rarified background.

Besides, I knew full well that Beryl Earnshaw's mother, who always wore classical type suits and a double row of pearls, would not be gadding about with a pork pie traveller on Speech Day. The other girls' mothers

were more for buttering up our headmistress and doing 'good works'. They were very boring really, the lot of them, but at eleven years old I stood in awe of them.

As we sang in the music room we looked out over the hockey field and tennis courts and could see Holy Trinity church in the distance, beyond the trees in the park. I felt to be in a truly hallowed place, enclosed in a magical world of music, where the future outside world of shopping and housework

Hilda Taylor in the early 1940s at about the time she was associating with the Pork Pie Man.

and the presence of Hitler, bombs and young servicemen's yearnings to be 'back in dear Old Blighty' and where Purcell and Bach were the reality. Those other things were but a vague happening in the subconscious. Even the forthcoming trauma of mother and the pork pie traveller receded into fantasy.

It being wartime with a scarcity of materials, we were sometimes encouraged to make our own musical instruments besides making the music. 'For homework this week girls, I want you to make a drum', Spikey announced authoratively one Monday morning. 'Get a pig's bladder to stretch across the body of the drum.'

We all chased down the winding staircase after the midday gong had boomed, wondering how on earth to get a pig's bladder before next week, yet all knowing that by hook or by crook we'd get them. Our school's motto was 'Honour Before Honours' so it musn't be achieved by foul means!

As usual with problems like this, I left the negotiations for my pig's bladder to dad. 'I'll see if Schofield (our village butcher), has one lying around'. Being on good terms with Schofield, by allowing each other extra rations whenever possible, my pig's bladder was duly delivered. Back home in my own environment, pride in my dad and the manner in which he could achieve the seemingly impossible, always put the posh girls' fathers in their lowly place. Well, lowly in my estimation. I knew their dads wouldn't be able to get them pig's bladders as easily as mine had.

Another time Miss Spikes said we had to make a violin for homework, dad managed to get a reasonable one made for me by a young soldier who was home on leave, in exchange for a couple of packets of cigarettes. He made it from bits of wood and lengths of catgut.

But in autumn, all our musical energies were focused on rehearsing the vocal programme for Speech Day. There was a big reputation to maintain. Choir practises were held during the last period on Wednesday afternoons. Though I adored the music and singing, it irked me to think of the rest of our form, those who hadn't passed the audition for the choir, being able to get their homework done, and not have a bulging satchel to take home. As the great day drew nearer, extra rehearsals were arranged. Music lessons began with enunciation practice, most important in Spikey's eyes. So we repeated 'Peter Piper picked a peck of pickled peppercorns, did Peter Piper pick a peck of pickled pepper corns? If Peter Piper picked a peck of pickled pepper corns, where is the peck of pickled pepper that the Peter Piper picked?' The explosions our lips had to make were almost as resounding as the anti-aircraft guns one heard on newsreels. My lips used to feel quite sore at the end of all that hard work! No wonder the local paper's music critic praised the 'clear and audible words.' It would have been a personal disaster for our Miss Spikes if every word could not have been heard at the very back of the hall.

During the war years Speech Day was held during the afternoon to avoid extra hazards created by blackout. We were advised to take torches with shades over their dim lights in case December fog and darkness fell extra thickly and early. One Speech Day we had just arranged ourselves on the tiered platform of Huddersfield Town Hall in our spotless white dresses and Brettle's lisle fawn stockings when the air raid sirens wailed. Miss Spikes was in control as usual. 'All go down into the room below until the all clear is given girls,' she commanded. 'Do not push and do not panic.' In the room beneath the Town Hall she continued her ebullient conducting. We crowded round her and defied Hitler by singing carols lustily.

Another year the mayoral party and other dignitaries and the head-mistress and her staff, all in their academic robes of office, walked up the side steps onto the flower-decked platform to be greeted with apprecia-tive clapping from the audience of parents. But as usual, the most thun-derous applause of all was reserved for our Miss Spikes, because everyone knew what a feast of delight she would have prepared for them. She too, in her way, was a vision of delight. Gone the sensible green tweeds and brogues. On those very special pre-Christmas Speech Days she was a splendid, somewhat Edwardian looking figure in floor sweeping black velvet dress and shoulder cape of white ermine with black dots on it. Beaming, she bowed to her ecstatic audience, secure in the knowledge that the repertoire of 'her girls' would bowl everyone over with their own special brand of Christmas magic. She and the choir, like the icing on top of the Christmas cake, were kept till last. First there were the speeches, sometimes dreary, occasionally witty, but not often. Always stressing the hope that the girls of Greenhead would 'strive to keep up the academic standards of those who would shortly be coming onto the platform to receive their School and Higher School Certificates. Then came the turn of the more athletic types who had earned their 'colours' for netball, hockey, tennis and swimming. I never did. Joan and I nudged each other and wondered if we were there purely for decoration, although we both did achieve our School Certificates in the fifth form.

House Shields were blushingly accepted by House Captains, and First and Second Year Girls who had shown most academic promise through the school year also received awards. Joan, my best friend and I, really felt to have been passed over. Then the prettiest and smallest first former tempered the austere dignity of those on the platform by presenting them with buttonholes. We were even too tall to be selected to do that.

The seriousness of an academic's speech was once the source of unexpected mirth when a Doctor So and So stood up and in his nervousness remarked how he had always wanted to see the sights of the town and one of the first he'd seen was Miss Hill (then our headmistress). Though severe in her flowing black gown dress and pince-nez, which frequently dropped on their delicate gold chain onto her ample bosom, even she had to permit herself a wry smile as the Town Hall shook to the gales of girlish and adult laughter while the speaker made pathetic attempts to rectify his faux pas. Such levity could only have been condoned in the festive season.

The Town Hall was noted for its marvellous acoustics and organ. One of the highlights of our Speech Day was a recital by the organist. Perhaps 'Sheep may safely graze', Bach's Chorale, 'Jesu, joy of man's desiring' or a short excerpt from 'The Messiah'. The sheer beauty of the music soaring to the lofty ceiling in the town hall often made me feel shivers of delight running up and down my spine. How I wished that all our customers could be there and not just parents of girls attending the high school. One can never adequately convey an ecstatic experience to others.

The head girl confidently read the lesson and the mistresses and school caretaker, the only male we ever saw about the place, were charmingly thanked for their work throughout the year.

Annie Hill, then headmistress of Greenhead High School.

Even the best tended form and house gardens won trophies in the Digging for Victory department! The results, vegetables and more vegetables, nothing as unpatriotic as flowers, were used in the school dinners, something I never stayed for, preferring to go home at midday to make sure that dad hadn't killed the pork pie man.

But at long last came the moment that everyone had been longing for, the carol concert by choir and school. First formers, not yet chosen for the choir, sweetly sang the rocking carol, 'Little Jesus, sweetly sleep, sweetly sleep, we will lend a coat of fur. We will rock you, rock you, rock you, we will rock you, rock you, rock you, we will love you all we can, darling, darling, little man'. Many a parental eye was furtively wiped before it was over. One of the ten year olds would then present 'Spikey' with a beautiful nosegay of Christmas roses which were accepted graciously before being placed on top of the grand piano on the platform.

When singing with the choir, 'Break forth, O beauteous heavenly light, and usher in the morning, ye shepherds shrink not with affright, but hear the angels waning…', I almost choked with emotion and despair at the sight of Dad, seated all alone in the audience, without mother, who was elsewhere engaged.

Then Peggy, the 'star' soprano of the senior choir, sang the descant in 'Angels from the realms of glory.' Amid that sea of white dresses, no-one in particular could be singled out as the soloist, unless they happened to know who it was, so I thought it was easy to imagine, as Peggy's voice floated on high, way up by the organ loft where she stood, that the voice really belonged to a celestial being.

It seemed to me that in so many people's lives at that time, there could be so little to worship.

Then the mood changed to a spanking, pacy 'God rest ye merry gentleman,' and 'The Holly and the Ivy.' Then, just for fun, 'Bobby Shaftoe,' sung fifty to the dozen, at breakneck speed, finishing to thunderous applause from appreciative parents. But the real *piece de resistance* that is still talked about to this day was when the whole school sang, with immense gusto, 'The Twelve Days of Christmas,' with actions. It did, as they say, 'bring the house down.' The sight of five hundred girls spiritedly pretending to be ten maids a milking and eleven lords a leaping (what thuds!) then when five hundred pairs of fingers were counted, held on high, for five gold rings, there was a near riot. Parents were not even satisfied after three encores, 'More!' they kept shouting, 'More!' Spikey was jubilant. Obviously thinking that all the hard work and painstaking hours put in beforehand was well worth the effort to bring such joy in a war torn world.

The junior choir charmed everyone with an exquisite rendering of 'Willie take your little drum,' (Patapan) beginning ever so softly at first as from a long way off, then increasingly loud singing and sounds of drumming before fading away again into the distance. Almost unearthly in its clear beauty was Peggy's solo 'In the bleak mid-winter' and the senior choir singing the old French carol 'Quelle est cette odeur agreeable?' (Whence is that goodly fragrance?). While 'A virgin most pure' was, one would imagine, an apt choice for a platform full of so many well brought up young girls. A Wassail carol also went down well – the one that has the words 'And here is to Fillpail and to her left ear, pray God send our Master a Happy New Year.'

To round off the event the audience was invited to join in 'Hark the Herald Angels sing', for, as one speaker commented, 'Speech Day would not have been possible without the parents in the first place.' For this part of the programme, and much to their delight, Miss Spikes turned her capable, ample back on the girls and vigorously conducted their parents. For me, Speech Day *was* Christmas, better even than Christmas Day itself. The magic of Christmas was captured more on that day, by singing all that festive music, far more than we ever heard on Christmas Day itself, and nobody was getting flustered and hot under the collar about cooking a garagantuan meal. All one's attention could be devoted to the glorious music.

How sad and 'down to earth' I felt when Speech Day afternoon was over, and five hundred temporary angels emerged from the Town Hall muffled up in gabardines, navy and blue striped school scarves, wellington boots and navy velour hats with navy and blue uniform hatbands. Parents paired up with daughters, I found Dad, in best Homburg hat and brave smile, waiting patiently for me in the driving snowstorm opposite the Town Hall. Neither of us mentioned mother and her absence with the pork pie man. It was too soon to break the magic spell we were still both caught up in. But later that night, when he thought Philip and I were fast asleep in our beds, we heard the sound of muffled sobs coming from his bedroom. I could have put the pork pie traveller's head on our bacon machine and sliced it off, without any qualms whatsoever.

TWENTY-ONE

Central Stores in Wartime

I felt to be growing up fast when I had my shoulder length hair cropped into the fashionable 'Liberty Cut'. A style innovated to be simpler for the girls in the Forces to wear beneath their uniform caps and for those in munitions to lessen the risk of catching long hair in machinery. Those who preferred to retain their long, page boy styles and sausage roll curls, wore things like fishing nets, called snoods.

My budding femininity came further to the fore when I used some of my clothing coupons to buy a fawn, teddy bear material, jigger coat. It had huge square, built up shoulders and gave girls a bit of the appearance of a walking bulldozer. Some shoulders were so wide two people had difficulty standing together at the bus stop!

I gave my notice in at the Building Society. I was bored stiff dealing with money, especially when I was relegated to the safe, to spend the day counting silver into bags. That job might be alright when you were old but it was not for me.

Lots of servicemen haunted Central Stores – like proverbial bees round a honey pot. Frequently, they stayed the night if they hadn't to be on duty the next day. There was no fuss and palaver about them staying like there is nowadays when guests stay. If they wore pyjamas there was always an extra pair of Philip's or dad's for them to wear. If not, a couple of blankets and a pillow were enough. If Central Stores had been a guest house it would have been called 'Free and Easy' or something like that.

Unlike other families, we had no worries about soap rationing. There was plenty in the shop, even if it was only red carbolic. Mother sometimes took a soldier to the theatre with her on a Monday evening, using the free pass. We were getting some marvellous shows then, as big stars were preferring to work in the provinces rather than in London. They felt safer away from all the bombing. One night my friend Margaret came with me to see *The Student Prince*. When we came home to the shop I made chips and fried onions for supper and discussed romance. It was romance then that girls were turned on by, not sex. Although it would have been wizard to have a handsome serviceman with me instead of Margaret, in one way it wouldn't 'cos I'd never have been able to have fried onions with a man – too unromantic.

Often, it seems, that when you're riding on the crest of a wave, something happens to put a damper on things. This happened to our family when poor Philip was struck down with meningitis. Just when he too was beginning to feel the first flutterings of romance and courting Betty, who'd joined the Land Army, in preference to the other services, so she would be nearer to him. She worked on a farm at the other side of town, near the moors and had become a dab hand at milking cows and haymaking. In off duty hours Betty sat with me, waiting on Philip hand and foot in the darkened room over the shop, ready to obey his every whim. But he didn't have any whims at all, except that the curtains remain closed and we didn't talk. We sat quietly mending clothes, or simply whispering to each other, or reading. Most of all we prayed he would live. What a relief it was, about a week later, when I was reading *His NAAFI Girl* on a chair by his bed, he stirred and murmured 'I

Hazel, wearing some 1940s fashions, with June Harries in about 1944. She made the handbag and lapel flowers from felt to save on clothing coupons but bought the jigger coat.

Two of Huddersfield's wartime 'glamour girls'
Dorothy and Barbara Brunt were customers at the
shop. They are with their father here at their house
in Bracken Hall Road, Sheepridge in 1945.

think I'd like to read for a while. Have you got today's paper? What's happening in the war?'

Before this Philip had laid like a log, white as death and the customers down below had kept their voices down and closed the shop door as quietly as they could. Whispering to Dad, Mother or Mildred as they came in 'How is he? or How is t'lad today?' I was downstairs in a flash and if it had been winter I'd have even warmed the newspaper first before passing it into those pale hands resting on the quilt. Then life picked up as Philip gradually began to improve. How could I ever have thought, even in the darkest moments, that one of we four at Central Stores could do such a thing as actually die, and leave the shop? How unthinkable and how stupid of me to ever have considered it. No, Mother and Dad and Philip and me and Prince and the seven cats, were all immortal. I didn't know how, but we were.

Then I was accepted by the School of Art as a full time pupil, and loved it. I also acquired a few boyfriends among the architecture students and went to the pictures with many of them. I remember going to see *For Whom the Bell Tolls* with Peter. As we sat holding hands in the one and nines, I was glad that it hadn't tolled for Philip.

Before he re-commenced work as a junior clerk at the National Provincial I recall Dad saying to Mother, 'I should hope we'll never argue again now that he's been spared. It'll be our Silver Wedding in another few years, we don't want to spoil everything now, do we?' They did stop rowing, for a few weeks, for Philip's nineteenth birthday. I bought him a record of Isobel Baillie singing 'Ave Maria' on one side, 'Oh for the Wings of a Dove' on the other. I'd be able to play it myself when he was out! But on his birthday the gladness was tinged with sadness as Grandma Haigh, mother's mother, died.

We perked up again quite soon after the funeral. There were too many interesting things to do to waste time in mourning. Though there was a war on, nay, perhaps because there was a war on, new faces, often extremely attractive ones at that, were constantly appearing at the shop and life was becoming more and more exciting. There were big stars on at the pictures, such as Sonja Henie, the new skating star in *Lovely to Look At*. How I longed to be able to wear one of those brief skating outfits and zoom about like a bird on ice, like Sonja did. I longed for big dimples like hers too. Huge ones, that appeared like deep pools in her plump cheeks when she smiled. Then we saw the romantic singing duo of Webster Booth and Anne Zeigler who appeared at the town hall in a concert. My friends at 'Tech' and I floated around in a romantic haze most of the time. Fully convinced that we'd come across Charles Boyer or Errol Flynn look-alikes among the soldiers, sailors and airmen that surrounded us at dances in the town hall and at the baths, which were turned into dance halls on Friday and Saturday evenings.

Life wasn't quite so rosy for Dad. Trying to placate customers hungry for something exotic in their rations, baking, dealing with points and ration books and increasing breathlessness due to angina. But it never once crossed our minds that the years at the shop were almost over! So we went on having

fun. I even had the thrill of speaking to Richard Tauber during the interval of a concert he gave at the town hall in December. 'May I have your autograph please?' I asked. He adjusted his monocle, took the book from me and scrawled his name. It was like a dream come true. Voices, and the words they say, have always inspired me more than the most handsome face could begin to do!

My village horizons were also enlarged with new girl friends that I would never have met had it not

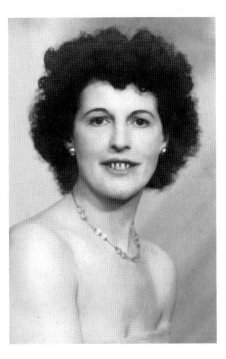

Hilda Taylor in a glamorous wartime portrait – 'main hobby flirting with soldiers and airmen who came into the shop for cigarettes'.

been for the war. Joan Bertram, a refugee from the Channel Isles, was billeted in a house near our shop and used to go dancing with me to the Baths. Our eyes sparkling more than ever if there was a famous Big Band playing, It seemed we were always inundated with partners. Being madly extravagant one afternoon prior to Christmas I splashed out five pounds, plus coupons, on a lovely black velvet dress. It had a deep 'V' neckline and I bought a bright pink cluster of feathers to wear at the bit where the cleavage was, or to pin in my hair for a change. No girl would have dreamed of wearing trousers to go dancing and we carried our dancing shoes in a brown paper bag, changing in the cloakroom when we arrived and paying our twopences in exchange for a ticket with a number on. We missed many a last bus home, having to queue for our outdoor clothes, which the middle-aged women behind the counter never seemed to be able to find.

As my appearance was of primary consideration then, I was seventeen and dreading being eighteen, I bought lots of brightly coloured felt, which wasn't 'on coupons' to make into pretty boleros and mittens. Then I embroidered my name on them, so no male could be in any doubt as to who I was. Having my name on view gave members of the opposite sex an opening conversational gambit, 'Hi, Hazel!' Then I'd blush and feign surprise that they knew my name. At that time I felt to be actually living out some of the songs I'd listened to as a child at the shop, tucked up in bed while mother and John pounded round the front room to strains of 'Goodnight Vie-e-enna'. One of my soldier boyfriends told me that he was born in Vienna. I couldn't pronounce his real name, so called him Vienna. It sounded ever so romantic. Of course, it was all in my mind. After a few dances with five foot nothing with a mouth wide enough to swallow a whale, and owlish glasses over a pointed nose, and me trying in vain to buckle my knees so I'd be nearer his height, I decided reluctantly that it wasn't him I was in love with, but his fancy name and where he came from. I've always been that way about names. I fall in love with the name first, not the body that owns it. So there was no chance at all of my becoming a Mrs Higginbotham, or Sidebottom, or Longbottom. No chance at all, even though the fellow himself might have been out of this world in looks. On the other hand, there wouldn't have been much point in going steady with someone who looked like the Hunchback of Notre Dame, even if his name was exotic, like D'Arcy or Churchill or something, though I'd have been sorely tempted, I must admit.

TWENTY-TWO

Going to Work

Part of our war effort at Central Stores must surely have been in helping to keep people's spirits up. Even in wartime there has to be humour or we'd all be dead. Not from bullets but from sheer monotony. So we sent lots of parcels abroad to John, and Jimmy, who used to be the baker, and to the other youths who used to pop in and out of the place treating it as a second home. We wrote airgraphs, keeping the lads up to date with all the silly things that still kept happening at the shop. Mother kept on patronising the Co-op hall, the Town Hall and the Baths, which held dances on Friday and Saturday nights and keeping the soldiers of the town in good spirits. Our colony of stray cats did their bit by keeping the mice down and therefore protecting the precious foodstuffs.

I passed the School Certificate and wanted to be an artist, but dad didn't think there was much call for those in wartime, 'what with paper being scarce and everything'. He thought I'd be better off in a job with some security, so I was plunged into the boring routine of office work at the ICI. I lasted three weeks, giving in my notice just as soon as I could. I returned to the shop every teatime after work, crashing through the door, cursing 'that stinking hole' while our customers stared after me, open-mouthed, as I slammed into the kitchen.

Next I began working at the Building Society in town and enjoyed that more. At morning 'break' time, being one of the juniors, I was entrusted with taking the orders for custards and jam tarts from the middle-aged ladies who had taken the place of male clerks, most of whom had joined up. I always got it wrong, bringing either too many jam tarts and not enough custards, or something else, from the little confectioner's in the arcade opposite. But the staff were civilised and pleasant and didn't object to swapping a custard for a jam tart to save hurting my feelings. I hated even the mathematics entailed in jotting up lists of jam tarts and custards, but no matter what mistakes I made, I made sure the manager got his order correct. He always wanted a custard!

I wanted to be an artist but it was wartime, and I couldn't be but there was still the escape of the cinema and the romance of it. *Now Voyager* with Bette Davies was 'wizard' in the parlance of the day and how I wept at *Goodbye Mr Chips*, starring Robert Donat and Greer Garson. Sometimes I'd take a 'date' to the theatre with the free pass if nobody else wanted it that week. I saw Ralph Lynn there in *Is your Honeymoon Really Necessary?*

It looked as though a bomb had hit the shop kitchen on the day men came to take out the Yorkshire range and fit a fawn tiled fireplace instead and it felt to be the end of an era. Grandma and Grandad had sat at either side of the Yorkshire range, pumping the fire into a blaze with the old pair of bellows. Now that was merely a memory, as so many other things, and people, were becoming at that time. How strange it felt to sit by that new sterile looking fireplace, listening to the wireless. Next day a customer was enrolled by Dad to paper round it, in exchange for a couple of packets of fags and a few jam tarts. Mother was still 'thick' with Sergeant Syme, and justified her friendship with him by throwing jibes at dad about his 'ginger bitch', while he tried in

vain to improve his increasing breathlessness by visiting a local herbalist every Monday. Wednesday was half day closing at the Halifax Building Society in Huddersfield, but we worked till five on Saturdays, well, the office staff did, though we closed before. It was longer if the cash didn't balance. I was the last to be able to leave, having to hang about until the books were correct before taking the postbag down to the Post Office.

Hazel at twenty-one on holiday in the Isle of Man in 1948 wearing her new 30/- bikini. She won the 'Miss Fenella' competition and this picture appeared in the Huddersfield paper – 'customers at the shop were agog!'

Hazel with Major in the field behind
Central Stores in 1948.

I enjoyed working on a Saturday though. Because that was the day we wore something special to go to work in, it being the weekend. Even though our dresses were covered, all except the front bit, by our regulation dark green overalls. Jigger coats were all the rage in 1944 and I wore mine with pride.

Mother now had a 'new' charlady from the council estate, Mrs Lee. She recruited her to escort her to the dances too, so she wouldn't be nervous going on her own in the blackout. 'Your husband won't mind,' mother soothed Mrs Lee's fears. 'He's in the army, how can he find out?' Even when the other grandma, who was still with us, mother's mother, came to stay at the shop for a few days, the dancing had to continue. Dad and I stayed in with the old lady, entertaining her with records while mother espoused the latest dance steps. She was mad about the tango.

As sweets were scarce I had a go at making 'Mintos', a new craze I'd read a recipe for in a paper. Mostly made up of strong peppermint cordial. We had lots of bottles in the shop. Grandma ate the lot, even though they didn't set as they ought to have done and she pronounced them excellent for her indigestion!

TWENTY-THREE

The End of an Era & a Wedding Reception

❦

Death is always a devastating loss and none more so for me than when Dad died of a heart attack on the eve of his Silver Wedding in 1948.

Maybe some of life's challenges are for the express purpose of diverting our attention from situations that otherwise could not be borne. The more ludicrous the diversion, the less one can dwell on the death, thus it was with the wedding reception.

The problem that loomed for Philip and me was a wedding reception booked at the Sunday school by Dad for Saturday 16 October. A wedding to cater for but the chief organizer, baker and chef that everyone relied upon, Dad, was not there anymore.

We hired a new baker, but his first offerings to our customers weren't greeted with the delight they had reserved for Dad's baking. This man's speciality was honey cakes. He churned them out by the score, batch after batch of them but nobody bought them. Nobody liked them. Our customers were used to Madeira loaves and fruit loaves on Mondays, Queen buns with icing and bits of cherry on top during the week and sponge sandwiches, light as thistledown, at weekends and, of course, Joe's gorgeous jam and lemon cheese tarts with pastry that melted in the mouth.

Frizby Dyke, as we had nicknamed our new baker, a little, harassed looking fellow with greying hair and furrowed brow, argued that making honey cakes saved the sugar. But that wasn't the point if no-one wanted them. It was embarrassing for us, then only twenty-one and twenty-three years old, to have to tell a professional baker in his fifties that nobody wanted his beloved cakes. He appeared to be mortally wounded when he was told and sulked for days. So how about the wedding reception menu? Dad had built up quite a reputation for being the very best caterer for miles around and we hated the thought of disappointing the newly wed couple on their special day. With Philip away at the bank all week it was even more worrying for me. I began to wish he'd cancelled it straightaway, while there was still time for them to get somebody else to cater for them. I received a very comprehensive letter, more like a list really, from Philip, a couple of days prior to the big day. Detailing what he thought would be suitable.

'I have not been able to get leave from the bank,' he wrote, 'so I shall not see you until Saturday.' My heart sank. Heavens above, me in charge of a wedding reception! 'I forgot to see Frances about making trifles. Will you ask her if she can possibly make them for me? There should be five trifle dishes in the cupboard in the kitchen and they should provide amply for fifty-six people. Ask her what she requires and let her have it. Cornflour, gelatine, margarine, sponge etc. They have to be ready for Saturday morning. Ask John (he was back from the army, working in engineering, but still a frequent visitor to the shop) what to get to go with the meat. He will be seeing you about it I suppose. Should you get salad ingredients from Tom Ramsden the greengrocer? (Ask John). He is seeing to the meat, knives and forks etc. Send eight white loaves, six brown loaves, eight brown teacakes, twelve white teacakes, three chocolate sandwiches (tell Frizby to ice them), two sponge sandwiches, five 1lb Christmas cakes, six Genoese cakes, three dozen jam tarts, three dozen French buns, four pints of milk, trifles, $1\frac{1}{2}$lb margarine, $\frac{1}{2}$lb tea, 3lb sugar, one jar of pickles, one jar of beetroot, one jar of red cabbage, (salad, if any), a packet of Saxa salt and one small tin of mustard. I think that is about all. Let John see this list and he will check it for you. Tell him I want it to be a good do, so I want to make sure that they get plenty, whilst we make a reasonable profit. If possible he will help to get the stuff all packed on Friday evening. Keep your chin up and keep the ball rolling. I shall be firing up the bakehouse oven again. I shall go to Audrey's for Saturday night. Our minimum price is £3,250 for anyone interested in buying the shop, house and bakehouse. Cheerio, Philip.'

For old time's sake, Frances and John, both former employees of ours, agreed to help in whatever way they could and without their moral and physical support I'd have been a bit like a worn out coalmine, ready to collapse at any moment, but they were by my side, stalwart and true as any pit props. Assembling the food was well under way on Friday evening, but none of the jellies would set. We all three stared at the gooey liquid in dismay. 'Chuck some more gelatine in,' suggested John, unceremoniously flinging in additional hands full into large basins. 'By God, Joe would have a right old laugh, if he could see us now.' There were no worries about the jellies not being set on Saturday morning on the wedding day of two of our best customers. It was just the reverse – they were as hard as rocks! 'Don't tell Philip,' laughed John, 'he'll have a fit and send any bills for broken dentures to yours truly.'

By mid-day, when we thought everything was under control, Frances came out with a bombshell, 'How are we going to get it all there and particularly that three-tier wedding cake?' None of us had given transport a thought. Taxis were too expensive, anyhow they wouldn't be able to fit the bakehouse trays inside one now that we'd filled them with food. None of us had a car and we certainly dare not risk carrying the wedding cake. Just then the shop doorbell tinkled and in strode the grimy faced coalman, shirt sleeves rolled up to the elbow, trousers with the top two buttons undone as usual, 'to give a bit o' breathing space.' His coal wagon was outside the shop square.

Stanley Griffiths (right) with his assistant Jimmy Ainley pose with the wagon that transported the wedding food in 1948.

Exactly as on that other Saturday afternoon, a few weeks before, when he had called to take Dad and Philip to the match. 'Gie us a packet o' cork tipped,' he grinned, white teeth showing whiter against his blackened face. 'The very man we need!' I yelled with relief and inspiration. 'If we pay you well, could you take some stuff down to the Sunday School for Dorothy and Derek's wedding reception? Have you time?' 'Aye, owt to help thi, I'd like to think I was doing a bit o' summat in memory of me old pal. And it won't cost you a halfpenny. It'll be my pleasure madam,' he grinned, whisking off his check cap and making me a low bow. 'Na then, thee be wrapping it all up, and I'll take me mucky sacks off t' wagon and leave 'em here till we come back. You're coming too, aren't you, to make sure nowt falls off, eh?'

With mounting excitement we carefully wrapped every item in tissue paper, sensing that a feeling of life and achievement was at long last beginning to radiate around the place again. 'I'll look after the shop till Philip arrives,' offered John, grinning from ear to ear as I clambered up onto the coal wagon alongside trays full of salad and cakes, buns, sliced meat, jars of pickles and all the rest of it. The wedding cake, well covered, was perched precariously in the middle of the trays. 'Happy landing,' called out John and Frances, waving us off from the shop doorway. 'Drive slowly won't you,' I shouted as Mr Griffiths heaved himself up into the driving seat. The whole wedding reception depends on you and me now!'

Operation wedding reception was pronounced a resounding success by one and all on the following Monday when Dorothy's mother called in at the shop. 'Your dad would have been proud of you,' she beamed, 'We had a right good do, thanks to you and Philip. So make the bill out and we'll straighten up.' That was something else neither of us had any idea about either. When Philip came home next weekend he suggested we look through dad's old ledgers to see if there were any indications as to prices there, for previous catering jobs. 'But I don't suppose he'll have entered what he paid the locals who acted as waitresses,' I replied. Still, whether we made a profit or loss is neither here nor there. The main satisfaction was that we had kept up the standards laid down by our grandad when he first started in business those many years ago.

We had kept faith with out customers, putting them first, given of our best, and gone out of our way to make sure no-one was let down at the last minute. We felt that this was reward enough and hoped that Dad would have been proud of us.

TWENTY-FOUR

What Next, Where Next?

Once the funeral was over, thought had to be given to what I would do and where I would live when eventually the shop was sold. Everybody else was safely fixed up but me. Philip was established in his banking career, engaged to be married and was welcome to stay at Audrey's home at week-ends. Syd's offer of marriage to mother apparently still stood, despite what she had or had not said to him on the evening of Dad's death. So she had somewhere to go when all the loose ends were finally tied up. But where would Spitfire, Hurricane, Cheeky, Ginger, Pussy Bakehouse, Major, the loveable black Labrador we brought when my old pal Prince died, and I go? I'd though about joining the WRENs because navy suited me best, then dismissed the idea because I didn't think they'd accept five cats and a dog besides me. But that was before the vet 'put them to sleep.'

I'd toyed with the idea of living with mother and my step-father to be but more out of desperation than enthusiasm. But for the time being, all my energies had to be directed to dealing with the shop. Making it appear a desirable residence, polishing the old furniture up, keeping the counters and shelves clean and tidy, putting down mouse traps all over the place, hoping beyond hope that when prospective buyers came they wouldn't be put off by squeaks and strange rustling sounds along the shelves. Mice weren't as frightening in the daytime as at night, and I lived in mortal fear of having to sleep in that house and shop entirely alone. Obviously mother didn't relish the idea of her new husband and me living beneath the same roof so she suggested I could live with his old widowed mother, in a part of the town I didn't care for at all. I was desperately worried. Part of me wanted the shop sold quickly, so we could all get on with the rest of our lives, the other part of me dreaded it. It would sever all my old links, with what had been a safe and secure exis-

Audrey Cudworth, Philip's wife to be, dressed for work at the National Provincial Bank in Westgate.

tence. If I didn't enjoy a job, I knew I could throw it up and live at the shop without any worries about where my next meal was coming from. All that would soon be over.

By mid-October mother was gradually winding down normal life at the shop. Most of the time she was living at her new home and the wedding was fixed for November. She had the carpets lifted from the upstairs rooms and removed to her new abode and life at Central Stores became a miserable affair. Mother put everything she could come across into the shop to be sold off. There was a constant sale of books, ornaments, chairs, even some of the old cardboard boxes from drapery drawers filled with old fashioned shirts and a few forgotten flannelette bloomers were all put out for sale.

TWENTY-FIVE

Mother's Wedding Day

When the excitement of *that* wedding reception was over, the stark facts of my situation came to the fore again. 'You go to live with mother and that murderer and I'll never speak to you again' Philip announced, when I remarked that I dare not sleep at the shop alone. And what if Mavis or Jeanne couldn't come one day? What then? It was alright for him, he had two places to go to. His comfortable 'digs' and Audrey's house. How easy it is to be moralistic when the problem isn't one's own. 'I don't know how you can even consider it, have you seen the balances in the books? They show hardly any profits at all! Mother's been dipping into the treacle well all these years, she never thought it would eventually run dry, did she? So you and I won't be able to get anything like what we ought to have had. Imagine, Dad killing himself with work and that other B....... reaping the benefits.' Although dad had died intestate, mother still would have the bulk of what there was.

Time wore on up to Thursday 11 November, Armistice Day, the day selected for mother's new wedding day. It was hardly a peaceful affair. Philip was determined that it would not be. This time there was no white dress and orange blossom but in order to have something new she had had a grey army blanket dyed red and a local dressmaker make it up into a warm winter coat for her. She could have done with a gun too, besides an army greatcoat. As she set out from the shop to walk down the hill to the bus stop, *en route* to the Registry Office in town, Philip dashed upstairs and flung open one of the bedroom sash windows. It was a foggy day and bitterly cold. I was serving customers in the shop when suddenly there was such a hullabaloo from upstairs. 'Don't think you'll get away with it this time,' Philip's voice boomed out as we dashed into the road to see him hanging over the windowsill brandishing a gun. 'I'll be outside that Registry Office waiting for you both when you come out.' There was more yelling, then the window was slammed shut.

'Ee, what a carry-on in't it?' grinned old Mrs Muffett. 'Ah do wish you weren't selling up. It'll be dull as 'ditch watter' wi' somebody else in charge o't old place.' 'Can't you change your mind Philip, give up the bank and take this on lad?' someone else suggested. 'No fear,' he panted, out of breath with his ranting and raving, 'I'll be glad to get away from all this.' 'Tha did give us a shock,' Mrs Muffett remarked appreciatively, 'Ah allus thowt tha was a reet quiet young lad!'

'So I am, Mrs Muffett, so I am,' he grinned, twirling the toy gun in his hand.

In those five minutes there had been more verbal fireworks than all the real fireworks we'd sold on Bonfire Day. With Philip hurling all the insults he could think of for what he considered mother's 'betrayal' of dad's memory, so soon after the funeral. He went into the kitchen and returned, putting on his coat and wrapping a warm scarf round his neck. 'I don't know how long I'll be', he said, 'I'm off into town now, on a bit of business.' D'you think he'll kill 'em?' Mrs Muffett wanted to know, full of eagerness about this latest bit of drama. 'What, with a toy gun?' I quipped, opening the till for her three shillings and sixpence. 'What time is there a bus up into town?' she asked, 'I think I might pop up there and have a look around.'

She was back in a couple of hours, laughing so much that tears were running down her lined face. 'Oh, what a laugh! Oh my goodness, I've never seen anything as funny in all my life. Your Philip was walking around the outside of the Registry Office with a really grim expression on his face, one hand in his coat pocket. Then he hid behind a corner

Hilda and Syd Gregory on holiday in 1949.

Hilda in the garden at Cowlersley after her marriage to Syd in 1948.

and that there pal of your mother's, Mrs Davidson, suppose she was there as a witness, came dithering to the doorway, all done up to the nines with a carnation in her buttonhole an' all. She tip-toed all round the building, looking all over for the enemy. I could see that Philip was busting with laughing, fancy your mother pushing her out first! She was determined that if there were going to be any bullets flying around, they weren't going to be meant for Hilda. I'll say this for her, nobody can be bored when she's around. Oh, let me sit down on't chair, bring us a sup o' water lass, believe me, it was better than going to't pictures.' I had to smile, despite my mixed feelings. What a contrast to that earlier wedding, garbed in a blanket for a coat, no congratulations, no presents and a son, usually a model of decorum and impeccable behaviour, hurling insults and lurking about with a 'gun', and certainly this time, no wedding bells.

TWENTY-SIX

A New Way of Life

~⁊~

Desperate to cling on to any vestige of my former life, I accepted the offer to live with Mother and Syd, my new step-father, and Major the family dog. How ever could I have left Major? How strange it was to live in a private house and not a bustling shop and for mother to be a customer and not behind the counter. Having to carry groceries along the street and not simply to be able to 'nip into the shop' and get whatever she wanted. Living there at first was awkward but Major was my ally. I could always talk to him and even Syd loved taking him for walks.

I began working at David Brown's Gear manufacturers, in the despatch department. It was within walking distance, up the fields to Crosland Moor. Dreams of becoming an artist vanished, as did life at Central Stores. When Barbara Mitchell, Margaret Sykes and the others went to the Tech' in the autumn of 1949 for book-keeping, shorthand and typewriting I was not the slightest bit interested in those but was intrigued by the Free-Lance Writing Course. I remember being amazed that anyone could be paid for writing letters to magazines and newspapers. I had always adored writing and expressing my thoughts in diaries or the long letters written to boy friends during the war. Perhaps if people converted their angry feelings into writing instead of physical violence the world might be a happier place for everyone.

I couldn't believe it when a cheque arrived from the *News Chronicle* one day – a whole guinea for a five-line letter! From then on I was hooked, writing became my solace and provided an occasional financial boost.

I had boy friends but it seems they were often quickly despatched. Then Christmas 1949 arrived and I went to a dance at Cambridge Road Baths. I wore my new grey Chinchilla fur cost, bought from proceeds of the shop winding up, black velvet dress and 'Evening in Paris' perfume but there was no Prince Charming. On the last bus home a leering, beery drunk plonked himself down on the seat next to me. The handsome, young bus conductor came for our fares and I recognised him as the young man I'd noticed on the top deck of a trolley bus some days before. He had dark brown eyes and I had felt a kind of tension between us then but no words had been spoken. I remember being vaguely disappointed he was only a bus conductor, especially as something seemed to be telling me that 'I will marry this boy'.

Dad had had great ambitions for Philip and me. Philip he was not too worried about but 'Hazel', I overheard him saying once to Auntie Annie when she came for her rations, 'was an enigma'.

I may never have encountered the bus conductor again, but as I alighted at my bus stop, where the drunk was getting off as well, I said to him that I was afraid of where the drunk may be going. Chance meetings so often shape our futures! 'Would you mind waiting with me until I see which way he is going?' I ventured. He gave me a quick, kind smile that I was to know so well in years to come. 'Hop back on. The bus is going back to the depot now, I'll see you home', offered Granville, as he introduced himself, 'And you are – ?' 'Hazel Taylor and I'm twenty-two. How old are you?' 'I'll catch you up on January 13th', he grinned. He'd been born on Friday 13 JAnuary 1928.

Arriving outside 41 Avison Road where I now lived we learned more about each other. Granville had wanted to go to sea and had trained at Trinity House, but to his disappointment couldn't continue because he was colour blind. After a time in the Royal Signals he now had no job so he was working on the buses until he decided what to do next.

In the early hours of Christmas morning, as we talked on and on, Granville suddenly asked 'Will you marry me?' If a bomb had exploded between us I couldn't have been more astonished. His eyes were sincere and his voice also. 'I mean it, I knew the first time I saw you, you were the girl for me.' I declined an invitation to meet his family next day. I didn't want to spend the rest of my life in the Colne Valley with a man on shifts, leading a humdrum and ordinary life. Now, married to a gipsy maybe, that really would be romantic. A camp fire, a few happy mongrels, songs by the light of the moon – 'Oh play to me, gipsy, the moon's high above, oh play me your serenade, the song I love'

Granville was not deterred. He'd do anything, he said, change his job, grow a moustache (thereby enhancing his resemblance to film star

Ronald Colman) and dispel all appearance that he might be seven months younger than me, even to be called 'Gipsy'. He refused, though, to wear a silk necktie, gipsy fashion, instead of an ordinary tie.

It was not until later when I saw him on stage in a production of *Merrie England,* in 1951, as a lord-in-waiting, looking devastatingly handsome and romantic (I'd never seen his legs before) and singing 'Rose of England' and, my favourite, 'For Your Caresses' that I finally accepted 'a little ring' and knew my future was bound forever with his.

We were married on 2 October 1952, on a Thursday, thinking that to be far superior to the common or garden Saturday wedding. Unfortunately it rained non-stop, while the following Saturday was a heavenly, Indian Summer type of day.

We couldn't afford to go anywhere, but I didn't mind, we could hardly wait to move into a home of our own. Our reception was at Fields Café for 6/6d a head. I bought the vocal score for the musical *Bless the Bride* for the evening planned at my future-in-law's home. Excitement came, not from expensive gifts, but from getting together enough household goods to live in our terraced home. We put down a deposit of £200, from my late father's will, and wondered if we'd ever pay off the £1,350 remaining on the mortgage.

Auntie Annie gave us a brass coal scuttle which we gleefully transported to Fenton Road on the bus. Cousin Winnie sent round a removal van with a single bed, a dressing table and a chest of drawers as her wedding present – she was buying new ones. What fun it was writing a list of what we had and what we needed when we could afford it. Included on this list was half a dozen whisky glasses, 'No use until we've got more money', I wrote alongside it.

We had a mattress for the double bed from mother and I bought a Welsh dresser dining room suite with 'Utility' marks under the chairs. We couldn't afford a wireless but I'd given Granville a musical cigarette box, which played the Harry Lime theme

Granville Wheeler at about the time he met Hazel.

125

Wedding day for Hazel and Granville, 2 October 1952. On the left are, Margaret (Granville's sister), Gilbert and Elsie (his parents) and on the right are Philip, Hilda, Eric Schofield and Audrey.

tune, for a birthday present – at least we'd be able to keep lifting the lid and listening to that! I had my vast collection of 78's, including Richard Tauber, Heddle Nash, Webster Booth and Anne Zeigler – heaven!

The house where we were to both honeymoon and live had only a basement, cellar kitchen leading onto the back garden, but no such refinements as fitted cupboards.

Some people in the terrace had their ovens in the living room upstairs, but I wanted a separate kitchen, despite the inconvenience of having to run up and down steps every time we needed something.

In 1952 Granville was earning £7 a week in the shipping department of Hopkinson's valve makers and our mortgage repayments were £7 a month. The wedding flowers cost more than a week's wages. No wonder we decided that one wedding in a lifetime was costly enough, and 'till death do us part' a more sensible proposition!

My crinoline wedding dress cost £31 from Leaders of New Street. The assistant made me practice walking in it, kicking the voluminous folds out in front, a bit like a goose-stepping soldier. I kept the gown on all evening as I wanted to get my money's worth out of it, besides, it was only once in a lifetime.

Mother played 'Bless This House' on the piano, and Philip, who had a deep baritone voice, sang excerpts from *Bless the Bride*. We told anecdotes about other people's wedding days and wondered where we would be fifty years on. I was glad in a way not to have the bother of wondering what to pack for a honeymoon. All that paraphernalia of trains and so on and how would Major have borne not seeing me for a whole week?

It was midnight when a friend transported us to our first home. We couldn't imagine what it must be like to own a car. My new husband gathered me up, smothered in white crinoline, and carried me over the threshold into the uncarpeted abode. He couldn't have been the Gipsy if it had been more luxurious! We hadn't any curtains either but we didn't think the neighbours would go so far as to be peering in at that late hour.

Next morning the sun was shining and I went into the basement to cook our first breakfast, taking the black pudding and kippers out of the green meat safe which looked a bit like a rabbit hutch.

The family group at Windsor Road, Cowlersley in 1984. Back row, left to right: Granville, Audrey Taylor, Philip Taylor, Syd and Hilda. Front row: Shirley Taylor, Caroline Wheeler and Elizabeth Wheeler.

Breakfast on the tray I went into the garden and plucked one of the last red roses of summer. Not possessing a vase I put it into an empty jam jar on the tray to mark our honeymoon.

A neighbour, Mrs Blackett, banged on the door. We heard her laughingly bawl out to someone, 'They're not up yet, they must be enjoying themselves'. I was mortified and wondered how I'd face the outside world again after black pudding and red roses in bed at ten o'clock in the morning.

My new husband spent the morning energetically trying to remove the rust from an old frying pan we'd been given. It saved buying one. After that we walked into town to buy groceries and even the pavements felt different now I was no longer a single girl. It was unreal when I was first introduced as 'my wife Hazel'.

Next day I joyfully baked some cakes while Granville dug the garden over and we left the cellar door open so we could talk to each other. In the afternoon Audrey, my bridesmaid, and her mother arrived with two pillowslips as a gift and enough boiled ham, tomatoes and lettuce for us all to have tea.

Next day my neighbour, Mrs Kaye, bustled in to show me how to starch my new husband's shirts and how to bake bread. What a delight that October teatime was when Granville came home and we had new made bread with home made blackberry jam, seated at our little coffee table made from a couple of orange boxes. That afternoon I had spent over £3 from my bank account on an armchair and the assistant at the shop had invited me to watch a big train crash on television. I had never seen television before. We shared the luxury of this one armchair for some time before we could afford to buy a second one!

Philip, mother and Syd eventually became good friends and we all settled into our new lives. Granville and I had two daughters, Elizabeth and Caroline, and Syd was overjoyed when they called him 'Grandad'. He became very fond of them both and loved having them stay for weekends and taking them on holiday. Philip moved to Great Yarmouth where he became a bank manager but we stayed on happily in Huddersfield where Granville became the shipping manager for English Card Clothing at Lindley.

The book began with customers at Central Stores who depended on getting things 'on tick' but as we go through life most of us find that we depend on others for help and support at some time, and in different ways, so I suppose in this sense we have all, occasionally, 'Lived on Tick'.